T0381188

Zimbolicious Anthology:

An Anthology of Zimbabwean Literature and Arts,

Volume 3

Edited by Tendai Rinos Mwanaka

Mwanaka Media and Publishing Pvt Ltd,
Chitungwiza Zimbabwe

*

Creativity, Wisdom and Beauty

Publisher:

Mmap

Mwanaka Media and Publishing Pvt Ltd

24 Svosve Road, Zengeza 1

Chitungwiza Zimbabwe

mwanaka@yahoo.com

https//mwanakamediaandpublishing.weebly.com

Distributed in and outside N. America by African Books Collective

orders@africanbookscollective.com

www.africanbookscollective.com

ISBN: 978-0-7974-9645-3

EAN: 9780797496453

DISCLAIMER

All views expressed in this publication are those of the author and do not necessarily reflect the views of *Mmap*

Table of Contents

iii

About editor:

Tendai Rinos Mwanaka is a publisher, editor, mentor, thinker, literary artist, visual artist and musical artist with over 20 books published. He writes in English and Shona. His work has appeared in over 400 journals and anthologies from over 27 countries, translated into Spanish, French and German. Find his books here: *http://www.africanbookscollective.com/authors-editors/tendai-rinos-mwanaka.*

Bio Notes of Contributors

I am **Sheila Banda**, 35 years old. A wife and mother to two boys. I am a librarian at National Free Library in Bulawayo. Currently staying in Bulawayo and studying towards a degree in Library and Information science. Passionate about writing, my icon being Tsitsi Dangarembga.

Yeukai 'Mimyie' Benhura is an aspirant writer from Zimbabwe. Her favoured themes are family and women empowerment. She is a member of Zimbabwe Women Writers and Poetritis Nirvana organizations that work to empower writers.

Nyashadzashe Chikumbu is a Zimbabwean born Poet, satirist and writer. He edits for Writers' space Africa and sits on the advisory board of African writers development trust. Chikumbu is also a member of the Indigenous African languages Association.(IALA.)

Phumulani Chipandambira is a freelance writer who lives in Norton, Zimbabwe. He likes reading and writing short stories and poems. His works have been published in various local magazines, blogs and newspapers.

Simbarashe Chirikure was born in 1974 at Musami Hospital, Murehwa District, Zimbabwe. He attended Zengeza 8 Primary School, and Zengeza 2 High School, Chitungwiza. He attained qualifications in Supervisory Management at Management Training Bureau, Masasa, and a Diploma in Business Leadership with the Zimbabwe Institute of Management. Some of his poetry is published in *Hodzeko Yenduri* anthology.

Troy Da Costa says, "It is with feelings of humble fortitude and privilege I once again get to contribute to this worthy project. I hope it inspires poets of all ages to engage in the mathematics of language to create beautiful work to showcase the vast and enigmatic culture of Zimbabweans. If anything is to be learnt from the events of the past year it is we as a nation can no longer walk head low and silent, we are brightly coloured flowers and we deserve to shine. Writers and poets of skill and passion can mirror our society and effect change by showing its ills and illuminating its strengths. This is your task and your duty and the reason art and literature exist.

John J.J Dongo is a researcher, blogger, poet, spoken word artist. He started writing at an early age and has been a lover of the arts and the power that they have to touch lives and positively impact them. He is the current country representative of The Human Projects.

Born in South Africa in 1947, **John Eppel** was raised in Zimbabwe, where he still lives. His first novel, *D G G Berry's The Great North Road,* won the M-Net prize and was listed in the Weekly Mail & Guardian as one of the best 20 South African books in English published between 1948 and 1994. His second novel, *Hatchings,* was shortlisted for the M-Net prize and was chosen for the series in the Times Literary Supplement of the most significant books to have come out of Africa. His other novels are *The Giraffe Man, The Curse of the Ripe Tomato, The Holy Innocents, Absent: The English Teacher, Traffickings,* and (awaiting publication) *The Boy Who Loved Camping.* Forthcoming from Mwanaka Media and Publishing is a collection of stories and sketches, *White Man Walking.*

Natasha Tinotenda Gwiriri was born on 14 May 2000 at Bindura. She attended Maneta Primary School, Buhera, Zimbabwe, and then Mutambara High School, Chimanimani. Meanwhile she is doing Advance Level at Chipadze High School, Bindura. She is interested in writing poetry and is still experimenting with other literature genres.

I'm **Andrew Huje**, born in Mazowe on the 27th of May 1993. I went to Kushinga Primary School for my primary education and went to Chiswiti Secondary School in Mt Darwin and Rujeko High School for secondary education . I started writing poems in 2011 doing my 'A' level.

Lisa Jaison: I was born in the city of Gweru in Zimbabwe. After my first degree at the Midlands State University I relocated to South Africa where I commenced a carrier as a research consultant, and studying for my post grad with the University of South Africa. I remain an avid reader and an artist at heart.

Nkosiyazi Kan Kanjiri is a South African based Zimbabwean poet. He was second (winner'sloopf) Drama For Life National Online Poetry Contest held by the University of Witwatersrand in 2017. Some of his poems are featured in *Eagle On The Iroko*, an anthology published in Nigeria in memory of Chinua Achebe.

Christopher Kudyahakudadirwe is a proud Zimbabwean freelance writer who believes that the only way to continue speaking to people even after one has departed to meet the ancestors is by writing. Period.

Shingirai Manyengavana is a 2017 Outstanding Poet National Arts Merit Awards (NAMA) Nominee, Published Prolific Writer and Vernacular Spoken Word Artist who is based in Mutare, Zimbabwe. Shingirai Manyengavana also scooped an award as the First Runner-Up in the Poetry Category in the Starbrite Talent Search Show Class of 2013. Shingirai is also one of the collaborators of the ZJC Shona Poetry Set book *Gwatakwata Renhetembo* 2016.

Blessing T Masenga is poet and an activist currently in exile since 2008. Through his poetry he often seek to reveal the misrule of failing governments and the violations of basic human rights that the press are afraid to give publicity to.

Mandla Mavolwane: I am a student currently studying Psychology at the Midlands State University. Writing poems is a form of therapy and it also helps me to express my views on the events that take place in daily life.

Cecil Jones Myondela better known as **Chenjerai Mhondera** is a writer, poet, performer, song composer, playwright, humorist... He has published several books, published in many anthologies; all series of *Best New African Poets*, *Zimbolicious*, and *Mupakwa weRwendo*, also published in online journals, magazines and blogs. He is a Patron and Founder of Young Writers Association (IWA)which helps to nurture and publish young and emerging writers. He is a citizen of the world, comes from East and lives in Zimbabwe.

Oliver Mtapuri is a Zimbabwean academic working in South Africa. He has published a number of academic books and several journal articles. He ran *Jive Magazine* for a number of years in Zimbabwe. Oliver has contributed poems to a collection titled: *Poetic Encounter: Rhapsodies from the South*. He writes about anything worth writing about. For as long as Oliver can imagine, dream, hope and aspire, he will keep on writing. Oliver passionately believes in African unity.

Tinashe Muchuri blogger, award winning journalist, performer, poet, storyteller and writer based in Harare. His poetry appears in several online and print magazines, Shona and English anthologies including *Zimbolicious Poetry Anthology Volume 1*. He is the writer of *Zvipfuyo Nevana Vazvo* and *Chibarabada*.

Jabulani Mzinyathi born 01.09.65 is a writer in general and at times described as a protest poet. He says he does not protest but is acting out of righteous indignation when he sees oppression in any of its forms. He had his poetry collection 'Under The Steel Yoke' published by *Mwanaka Media and Publishing*. His previous works have been published locally and abroad in several magazines, ezines and anthologies. Jabulani who calls himself a student for life holds a certificate in education, magistrates admission certificate, diploma in human resources management and a bachelor of laws degree. Having been a magistrate for twenty-one years Jabulani quit to become a lawyer in private practice at Beitbridge.

Thuthukani Ndlovu is a Zimbabwean spoken Word artist, born in Bulawayo and currently based in Bloemfontein, South Africa. He's the founder of *The Radioactive Blog* and *Giving Poetry Wings*. He's also the Vrystaat Literature festival Assistant coordinator, and has performed his work in Lusaka, Johannesburg, Cape-Town, Lesotho, Bulawayo and Harare.

Chido J. Ndoro is a fast rising poet who has contributed to a number of anthologies. She is a gender issues interventionist, bold and rustic. She is an observer of social injustices with a watch out eye for the development of mass consciousness. She is focusing on protest literature that addresses the political, social and economic issues in Africa. She also addresses women's issues, illuminating the difficulties women face in society.

Anesu Nyakubaya is a writer, blogger and poet. Her work has been featured in the *Zimbolicous Poetry Anthology: Volume 2* as well as *Divas Inc Zw's website* and a number of other blogs. In her words, inspiration is all around us and all we need to do is to concentrate, as her blog's tag line goes *life is poetry*. You can check out some of her work at www.soulfulmiss.co.za

Haile Saize- I, born December 15 1991 in Harare is a poet who expresses life ills by the power of a pen. Currently residing a self-exiled life in Cape Town due to economic hiccups in Zimbabwe. Studied Journalism and Media Studies apart from being an entrepreneur. Named Sydney Saize which he later changed when he gravitated towards Rastafari, citing that the name is of western origin. His poems are published in the *Best New African Poets 2017 Anthology, When the*

Baobab Fall, an e-book collection of poems tribute to Morgan Tsvangirai among other great poets and also published in the *Miombo Publishing*.

Bruno Shora is a rising academic/writer who has so far published a research paper in an academic journal. He also has several other research papers and a book which are still under consideration. Bruno has developed a kin interest in what has come to be known as Peace Studies. It is through writing that we can also peacefully express ourselves, not with stones, not with fire and not with guns. Through poetry, we also find an escape route from the vagaries of this world. Bruno Shora is a holder of a Bachelor of Arts Degree in English and Communication Studies, Master of Science Degree in Peace, Leadership and Conflict Resolution and he also looks forward to soon embark on Doctoral studies.

Moreblessing Size Tafireyi is a poet, writer and librarian from Gweru now based in Harare. She has performed her work on various platforms in Harare such as Shoko Festival, Intwasa Arts Festival and at the Free State Literature Festival 2018 in Bloemfontein, South Africa. Some of her work is being currently published in print and online.

Michael White born on 18th of June 1997. I did high school at Oriel Boys High School where my literature teachers as was my favourite subjects encouraged me to pursue writing and public speaking. Writing poems is my way to subside my emotions during my emotional moments and also is my passion. My aspiration is to one day publish an anthology

Thamsanqa Wuna is a 27 year old Accountant and entrepreneur with a Bachelor of Business Administration degree from Solusi University. A human rights activist and gender equality advocate, he is keen on protest poetry with particular focus on the Zimbabwean perspective. He is an avid reader and he will always find time to read a book.

Learnmore Edwin Zvada is a Zimbabwean born poet who resides in Harare, the capital of Zimbabwe. Some of his poems have appeared in online magazines, namely, *Duane's PoeTree, The Literary Yard, Tuck Magazine, Dead Snakes* and *Whispers.* Two of his poems were featured in *Zimbolicious Poetry Anthology, Volume 2.*

Introduction

After *Zimbolicious Poetry: An Anthology of Zimbabwean Poets 2016*, which we have republished as *Zimbolicious Poetry Anthology, Volume 1,* in 2018 and *Zimbolicious Poetry Anthology, Volume 2* of 2017, the Zimbolicious project enters the third volume of the series as *Zimbolicious Anthology: An Anthology of Zimbabwean Literature and Arts, Volume 3.* It has 5 short stories, 51 poems, 1 nonfiction piece and 3 drawings from Zimbabwean writers and artists. We have considerable work in Shona language but little others from the other indigenous Zimbabwean languages unlike the previous two offerings. We decided to expand the anthology to encompass many other Zimbabwean arts like fiction, nonfiction, visual art etc, and we hope in the future these will strengthen as the poetry genre has done.

Zimbabwe still tumbles on its unshakable political trajectory with quite a lot that has happened since our last offering. Last year, that is 2017, we saw our oldest man of politics, Robert Mugabe, removed through a military coup, and a lot of writings in this anthology addresses this and the hope from the Zimbabweans for a free and fair election in 2018. As I write this introduction we have had another polarized and highly fractious election that was decided at the courts. There are a lot of questions, angers, mistrusts we don't have answers for about the enigmatic political landscape that Zimbabwe is and the Zimbabwean people are. I hope this anthology has lifted the curtain to show a bit of the answers, or discernible shapes or just the path to finding the answers.

We will continue moving on as a people despite our sharp political differences, and this anthology helps in mapping the way forward. The fact that we still get together and address such issues in an anthology of art is positive. We need this.

Despite our political problems we have a lot to celebrate about our humanity as a people and the poets highlight a lot other of these issues, issues to do with love, morality, spirituality, tradition, relationships, family, identity, the individual- with joy, hunkering, sometimes with peace and satisfaction.

Fiction

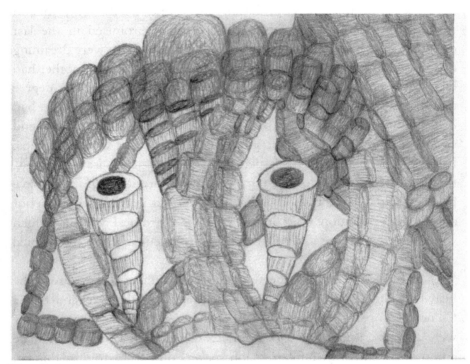

He Cries

Artwork © by Tendai R Mwanaka

The Deformed Dream

Christopher Kudyahakudadirwe

For a whole week now, you have been all over everywhere in the big city chasing after one of the two million phantom jobs that your president promised in the last elections. You had voted for him hopefully because you were dreaming of a good job after university especially after your widowed mother had literally closed her livestock pens in order for you to get the BSc degree that hangs proudly on the wall in your mother's sitting room. You had believed him without doubt that things were going to be on the mend and the economy would flourish birthing the jobs that would, perhaps, help to reopen the livestock pens of your mother. Disappointingly, three years into the five-year term of the old president, no jobs have been created for the millions of youths who are leaving school. Your anger and frustration boils inside you like a tropical volcano which would erupt any time as you trudge the potholed streets of the capital city.

On Monday, you had been to the light industry, just across the heavily polluted river, where you had heard over the weekend that a Chinese company was recruiting people to pack plastic toys that they were manufacturing. For four hours, you had waited outside the gate amongst the growing number of job-seekers only to be told by this fat, balding Chinese man that they wanted those with a BSc degree for the ten vacancies that were available. And you had forgotten your degree certificate at home. So, you were just like the others who had no education at all. You slouched away like a hyena whose kill has been taken over by a very hungry pride of lions.

Then on Tuesday you woke up before the sun showed above the eastern horizon and arrived at the site where the American Embassy

2

was constructing its new headquarters in the city. The contracted company wanted 'daga-boys' and you had remembered to take with you your BSc degree certificate just in case they wanted degreed 'daga-boys'. To your disappointment, the interview required that an applicant should be able to throw a brick high up to the second floor of the building. Your efforts, unfortunately, could not send a standard brick further than the first floor. It was a very disgraceful day especially when other young men like you were able to do with ease what you had failed to do.

Wednesday: another unfortunate day. A fertilizer company in the heavy industrial area wanted people to off-load a whole train that had hurled two hundred tonnes of fertilizer from the seaport into the country. These were 50kg net bags and you are only 47kg with your clothes and shoes on.

"You'll be paid according to the number of bags you will off-load," the foreman announced as soon as you were engaged. "This means you'll stack your bags in one stack and at the end of the day we'll count them. The more you off-load the more you earn. It's 50cents a bag."

No one was turned away. It was half past seven in the morning. There were men and women who had answered to the call for the job. The fifty-odd of you who had gathered for the job earnestly attacked the train like ants attacking the carcass of a dead python. The employer had assigned his permanent workers to climb into the wagons so that they would load the bags onto your heads and you would then carry them into the warehouse. So, when the first 50kg bag of urea landed on your dread-locked head, your knees buckled under you and before the bag crushed you under, you let fall to the platform and its powdery contents were all over.

"You're fired, boy! This work for men," the foreman was fuming as he shooed you out of the warehouse yard.

And that was the end of your job. All the castles you had built came crumbling on you like the bag of urea.

The previous day, Thursday, you spent it in First Street playing street soccer with other university graduates. The *WhatsApp* group message had requested you to come dressed in your graduation gown complete with the mortar-board, hood and rolled up papers to represent the certificates. The occasion was meant to be a statement-making get together to protest the president's failure to create the 2.2million jobs promised in the run-up to the 2013 elections. In attendance, the message said, would be the riot police, not those who quell riots, but those who facilitate it to happen (according to the term commonly used); the street vendors and those queueing for their money at the banking halls in First Street. So, you had cordoned off the area between HM Barbours and Ok Stores for the stadium. By eight o'clock, the place was bristling with the police in their egg-heads, brandishing glass shields and batons that quivered like the spines of agitated hedgehogs. The game was played and the media had a field day. The following day the police where blamed by the politicians for allowing you to denigrate the name of the president like that. Your story was the subject of a heated debate in the parliament between the ruling party and opposition party members of parliament.

Today is Friday. Some call it *Faraiday* – a day to be happy. It is the end of the week and people celebrate it in many ways possible. Those with extra money to spend go to the taverns and beerhalls to drown their financial problems with liquor and others go for *gochi-gochi* to kill their craving for grilled meat. These celebrations require financing. So, on Thursday evening when you heard about the grave digging jobs that had been created at Mbudzi Cemetery by an undertaking company, you were there before the sun licked the eastern horizon of the city.

4

"We want people who can dig at least three graves a day," the pot-bellied prospective employer bellows after several picks and shovels have been off-loaded from the white truck that immediately drives off.

There is a scramble for the tools. In this disorganised melee you manage to grab a pick and a shovel. The rule here, as you learnt later, is that those who have not been able to lay their hands on a tool have not been hired. You are happy to have secured a pick and a shovel. Those who would have managed a pick or a shovel only have to work together and that meant splitting the pay at the end of the day. While waiting for the truck to arrive word had circulated saying that the employer only paid those who would have dug three graves per day.

That way he was assured of finished graves since it was weekend, a time when most burials in the city were conducted.

Mr Pot Belly shows you where your work starts and ends. Soon sods of newly dug, sweet smelling soil are flying out and forming small hills next to the deepening rectangular holes you are digging. Diggers are getting shorter and shorter as the holes deepen. Shirts have been taken off and are flapping on the handles of the picks or the shovels depending on which tool is in use at any given time. The whole area looks like a sweet potato field where moles are busy burrowing and creating mounds of soil everywhere. This is work for a man and a half and not for those who attended school at St George's or Peter House.

By the time you are waist deep callouses have popped up in your hands; your back is aching and your throat is as dry as a desert; you cannot swallow any saliva because there is none to swallow. When you stop to take a rest, a lot of thoughts flash through your mind. You remember when you were at St George's doing your fourth-year secondary school. You were a brilliant and eloquent student to the extent that your English language teacher had drafted you into the debate club which was mainly an Upper 6 elite club. You were so good

5

at presenting your argument such that you became the opening speaker all the time you went for a debating competition. When you were in the Lower 6 you went overseas where you became the darling of audiences by beating the native speakers of the language. But then that was before your father's empire crumbled and he later died of stress resulting in your mother as well as you going to live in the rural areas

That was then and now after university you are facing the reality of your run-down country.

As the sun creeps to the zenith, you have not finished digging the first grave. Some of your fellow diggers are doing their second hole and others are starting on their third. Your hands are on fire. You dig for three minutes and take a rest of five. It would seem like you are not going to finish this one grave. The pain in your hands is very unbearable. You cannot bend your fingers to hold the handle of the pick anymore. But I'm an educated man, why should I suffer this way just like those who have not been to school, you ask yourself. Then what is the purpose of going to school if one has to do the work that an uneducated person can do? Who should answer that? You shake your head slowly as you contemplate whether to carry on working or quit at that moment.

The urge to quit overruns the one to keep digging. So, without telling Mr Pot Belly or anyone for that matter, you scramble out of the grave and you put on your shirt and head towards your aunt's house in the western part of the city. Two syllable words are spewing from your mouth as you walk away from the cemetery. You are cursing the day you were born: you are cursing the president of the country accusing him of blatant lying; you are so frustrated that you kick the stones out of your way. You blame the ruling party which created the situation that caused your father's companies to go under. You are so angry that you do not notice the shiny piece of metal that is revealed when you kick a stone out of your way until you are three strides away. Something tells you to go back and check what it is that is shining like that.

It is a folded $1 bond coin!

You pick up the deformed coin and brush off the little sand that clings to it. What could have made this coin to be folded like that, you wonder silently? You look at it carefully. No crack on it, right. Now many other things are crowding your muddled mind. It is Friday. A day when people celebrate the end of the week. At least I've somewhere to start from, you say to yourself as you quicken your steps towards the nearest bar. A $1 bond coin can buy you four litres of opaque beer. You are now feeling like a human being. Your gaiety is that of someone who has command of his destiny. The power of money! Isn't it the reason why people wake up early each day and run away from their warm and comfortable beds to look for, you muse as you enter the beerhall.

The noise in the beerhall does not reduce you to a beggar begging for masese from those who have the money to buy it. With exaggerated confidence, you walk straight to the barman.

"Barman, a two-litre pack of Super, please!" you proffer the folded $1 bond coin. You throat is already pumping like that of an angry frog.

The barman takes the deformed coin and looks at it.

"Sorry, we don't accept that kind of money." He literally throws it at you.

"But it's money, isn't it?"

"Not in this bar," the barman says as he goes to serve the next waiting customer.

All hope is gone. You pick up the deformed coin and go to sit at a table right in the darkest corner of the beerhall. You are afraid that he might think of calling the police and having you arrested for trying to defraud the beerhall. Alone in that dark corner, you listen to your hands throbbing and your back crack-aching and thinking: had the barman allowed you to buy with that deformed coin you would be wetting your throat with the thick Super which many people had christened: food and drink.

Then an idea dawns in your mind. You jump to your feet and quickly get out of the beerhall. Your legs take you towards the shops and surely there under the veranda, surrounded by boxes and boxes full of old broken shoes is the cobbler. He is busy applying glue to the sole of a shoe that he is repairing. The smell of glue is thick in the air around him.

"Excuse me, sir!"

The man looks up and then back at his handwork. "What is it, my son?"

"Can I use your hammer?"

"For what?"

You put your hand in your back pocket searching for the folded $1 bond coin. It is not there in that pocket. You check in the other and your hand comes out with it.

"I want to straighten this. The barman wouldn't take it like this."

The man continues applying glue to the sole of the shoe and you can see he has agreed to helping you. Then when he finishes what he is doing he stretches out his hand and you hand him the coin. He takes out his hammer and the cobbler anvil on which he puts the deformed coin. With two well directed strokes the coin is as good as new.

"Thank you very much," you say as you stretch your hand to receive the mended coin.

"Not before you have paid me." His whiskers are twitching like those of a cat that is preparing to eat a mouse it has just killed.

8

"How much?" you are calculating that if need be you will give him fifty cents and then you take the remainder to the barman and get yourself at least two litres of Super.

"One dollar fifty."

"Just for what you've done?"

"My charges start from one dollar fifty for any job that I do here, my son! So, you owe me fifty cents already if I keep this one."

You turn on your heel and walk away - dejectedly. When you turn around you see the cobbler caressing his goatie and a wicked smile crossing his lips.

Panhare naAmai

Oscar Gwiriri

Ndakaramba ndakanyarara nhare iri pachipfuva. Ndakange ndisisina remuromo kana zvekufunga. Ko ndaidiniwo kana ivo amai vaiita hasha dzakadaro. Payakati tywii, ndakabva ndazvambarara zvangu pamubhedha wandainge ndirere. Ndakatanga kurangarira nhaurwa yandainge ndaita navo, mwoyo wangu uchiita sewatsvetwa mudhiramu rizere mafuta anofashaira riri padarautsavana remoto.

"Mwanangu, zvauri ikoko ndiwe nharirire yedu. Baba vako vakashanya miviri yavo isina kubatana zvokuti takangoti hapana zvokuita, asi takazochena moyo apo takarangarira kuti gotwe ravo riri muJoni imomo. Baba venyu vakura ava, vave kungoshingirira zvavo kushanda, asi nyama hadzichada. Ngavatoende kubasa, ndivo vakada zvemhuri yakakura." Vakadaro amai panhare. Ndakashaya mashoko okutaura maringe nemashoko avo okugumisira.

"Pakanaka amai!" Ndakadaira.

"Ndinoda kuti uongorore zvakare zvingadaro zvichivanetsa, toita chirwirangwe kuvanyaradza nekuvasimbisa. Unozivaka kuti kana munhu akura kudaro, anonge oda rudo rwakanyanya, uye vanhu vane hanya pedyo. Saka ndiri kukupa basa mwanangu kuti tizive mudzi wechiri kuita kuti BP yavo igare yakakwira. Tikasadaro, anotisiya mudhara uyu. Kufa kwake zvinenge zvarova, musha unenge usisina chiremerera. Vana babamukuru nanababamudiki venyu munovaziva wani. Handiti ipapa baba vakadzoka, vose vanoti rururu kuita mudungwe kuuya pano kuri kuda kupihwa tunonaka. Chokwadi munhu anotadza kutotandadzana nemhuri yake semunhu ange asipo vanhu vakangoti pamu pamu mumba. Haa, zvekuno kumusha mabasa chaivo. Saka wazvinzwaka mwanagu, chengetedza baba. Rave basa redu tose

10

kuti tione kuti pfungwa dzavo dzakagadzikana. Tikasadzaro tinosara pachena."

"Ndazvinzwa amai. Asi sekutaura kwamaita kuti titsvage zvinetswa zvavo, pane kanyaya kandakaona kuti kanenge kari kuvafurufusha mupfungwa apo ndaitandara navo nezuro." Ndakanyevera.

"Hauchioni! Ndizvo chaizvo zvandiri kutaura kuti ngatiite. Chii chiri kuvanetsa?" Amai vakabvunza zvinyoronyoro zvokuti ndakanzwa rudo rwavo panhare zvisinei kuti ndaive kumhiri kwemugano wenyika kudaro.

"Pane nyaya yenyu yekutengesa mombe gumi kwamuri kuda kuita muchiti munoda kuvhakacha muchienda kuDubai kuri kuenda vamwe. Nyaya iyoyo iri kuvashun…"

"A-a! A-a! A-a! Wakatanga rini kupindira nyaya dzevabereki nhai iwe? Ndochii ichocho chauri kundiitira! Nyaya dzababa namai dzinopindirwa here iwe? Ndokupindiridza manje ikoko kwawave kuita, kupinda nemwenje mudziva chaiko. Ndosaka ndichigara ndichitaura kuti ndikafa vana imi hamuna rugare. Munotanda botso ndichiri mumba chaimo. Makaitwa sei, vana vasingade kundiona ndichifara?"

Ndakanzwa amai vachitura rino zibefu rakanditi bho-o pamoyo. Pavakamboti zii ndakafunga kuti zvimwe vadonha nehasha.

"Amai! Amai! Amai! Muchiripo here amai?"

"Saka unofunga kuti ndaendepi?"

"Ndine hurombo amai! Ndagara handipindiri nyaya dzenyu, asi…"

"Asi kuti watumwa nerwubaba rwako rwusina musoro ka?" Amai vakanyobvoka. Ndakashaya kuti ndingapotera sei, ndaishaya mashoko chaiwo chaiwo akakodzera ekuvapodza navo. Ndaiziva kuti amai chitofu chemarasha ekuHwange chokuti kana chabatidzwa, moto wacho haudzimwe nekuti fu-u sekanjera.

"Kwete amai!"

"Saka zvabvepi nhasi?"

"Ndangoti sezvo mange mati…"

"Kuti chii chacho!"

"Ndine hurombo amai, asi sezvo mange mati ndiite tsvakurudzo yezvinetswa zvababa ndabva ndangotaura chandakaona. Baba vari kuti dai mambomira nekuti mukatengesa idzodzo munenge mavhara danga mosara mombe mbiri chete zvo…"

"Iwe nababa vako musandisembure wanzwa. Ini handiteereri munhu. Rwendo irworwo hapana ari kuzorwuganura. Kana zvirizvo zviri kumurwarisa, kubva ngaafe zvake. A-a, handidi kufuwiswa nezvisina basa ini!" Amai vakaturazve zibefu. Hana yangu yakati dhii nemashoko avo seyadonherwa ikatsimbirirwa nenhurikidzwa yedzimba dzepamusoro pepandaigara. Ndakashaya mashoko akakodzera. Amai vakasimudzira zvakare, "Mombe idzodzo dzamave kukonorora muchiti pwedere pwedere, handiti dzakangotanga dziri mbiri chete, saka dzinongozadzazve danga racho. Iwewe une rimwero nababa vako ndakagara ndazviona, ndivo manyemwe emhuru iwavo. Ikodzero yangu semubereki kunge ndichikwidzwa ndege nemi vana vangu, asi hapana kana mumwe venyu anombotirimuka. Vamwe vabereki vari kuswera vari mvii mvii muchadenga, vana vavo vachiita kubvutidzana kuchengeta, asi ini mai nhiya woye kana siwiti haro, hapana. Ndinoita kunge ndakasara nezvisare ndarasa vana. Kubereka kwacho ndekupi manje ipapa. Ndizvo zviri kuitwa vamwe vanamai here izvozvo? Vamwe vangu kuchechi havadzokorodzi mbatya kwemwedzi mitanhatu chaiyo, asi ini ndinoita omandikupfeke. Vamwe vari zhimu zhimu mizvambarara yemotokari vachindityapwadzira madhaka, asi ini kana bhara zvaro rekuti ndikarwara ndinonzi nzenga nzenga imomo, hapana. Pane mubereki asingade kuchengetwa nevana vake here, ndozviudzawo aniko ini ndiri nherera? NaMwari o-o, hamufe makaona rugare vana imi nekuda kwezviito zvenyu! Sewe zvako, ndakakutamburira sei kukuendesa kubhodhingi ndichiti kana woshanda wozondiitirawo madanha, nyamba kwange kuri kurasa mari yangu. Dai ndakatokwira zvangu ndege kare zvange zviri nane. Ndochii chawakandiitira kuti kungopedza yunivhesiti, nekuroora iko kanzenza kako kaingonzenzereka imo muyunivhesiti menyu imomo. Tsve-e kufambaira chimwe, basa ndere kutsvaga varume. Baba anhiya wangu nekupusa ndokudyira nekutotora muroro kuunza pamba. Hero riri piriviri, shiri dzonetsa nekuda kudzomha. Saka kana ndozviitira hurongwa hwangu handide munhu anopinda munzira yangu. Uri kundinzwa! Handizvide izvozvo, chera kakomba uti ptu-u". Amai vakapopota. Ndakanzwa kuti tywii.

"Amai! Amai! Amai muripo here?" Ndakabata nhare ndokuipindurudza zvishoma nezvishoma ndichiitarisa zviye zvokunge ndiri kuda kuona amai ipapo. Ndakaedza kuvachaira nhare zvakare, asi nhare yavo yakange yadzimwa.

On line with Mom

Oscar Gwiriri

(Translated from shona by Oscar Gwiriri)

I kept laying handholding the cellphone whilst resting it on my chest. I was dumbfounded and my mind seemed to have frozen. Can you imagine how mom was so hash on me? When she cut off the line, that is when I threw myself on the bed. I started recalling the tele-conversation and my heart ached as if it was in a frying pan.

"Son, since you are in the vicinity of your father, we rely on you on his check up. You are quite aware that your father is always on-and-off healthwise, but he had to travel anyway. We were initially worried, but got consoled after realizing that you are in Jo-burg where he was travelling to. Your father is old enough to retire, though he keeps on going to work. Anyway, he has to work for his family. It was his choice to have such a big family," Mother proclaimed. Her proclamation shocked me.

"It's ok Mom," I said.

"You must keep an eye on him and try to ascertain whatever is troubling him so that we all take charge in giving him solace. I believe you are quite aware that people of that age need love and being cared for. Therefore, I am giving you a task to find out what could be irritating him resulting in this continuous hypertension shoot out. If we don't take that move, we will lose the man. Once he is gone, we will be doomed, and this family would have lost the father figure. You know how your uncles treat us. Just imagine, once your father touches ground here, they all flock into our house expecting gifts and presents. We rarely have our own time all because of their presence. I really wonder. Therefore, my son, take care of your father. It's now every

14

family member's duty to ensure that he is alright, otherwise the man will be no more."

"I get you clearly Mom. In reference to what you have said about identifying his worries, I have since noticed that there is something boggling his mind as we were relaxing yesterday night." I advised.

"That's it! You are quite on track on what I want us to do. What could be the problem affecting him, my dear?" Mother asked attentively. I could even feel her concern over the line.

"There is this issue about your plan to dispose ten cattle to raise funds for your holiday air ticket to Dubai. That issue is troubl…"

"What! Since when have you started interfering in parents' issues? What's wrong with you! How dare you get in between your father and me? You have gone out of bounds for sure. No wonder why I always caution you that once I'm dead, you will be in for it. My aggrieved spirit will haunt you for sure. Not even a single day have I ever got peace all because of you my children," Mother shouted. Her heavy sigh over the phone almost blasted my eardrum. There was silence for a while. I got worried that she could have collapsed out of anger.

"Mom! Mom! Mom! Mom are you there?"

"So you think I'm dead?"

"I'm sorry Mom! It's never been my intention to interfere in your affairs, but…"

"But what! I believe your damn stupid father could have influenced you. Isn't it?" She asked. I was lost of remorseful words. I knew my mother's behaviour quite well, once irritated; she could go berserk like a wounded buffalo.

"Not really Mom!" I answered.

"So what's all the fuss about?"

"I just considered that since you want us to know what's troubl…"

"What?"

15

"I'm so sorry Mom, but as you had advised that I must find out what's bothering father, then I just thought it's one of them. Father was suggesting that if you could hold on for a while so that the cattle multiply, than disposing the ten out of the dozen which…"

"You people don't irritate me, okay! I am not going to listen to any of you at all. As far as I am concerned, that Dubai trip is an obvious and unstoppable whirlwind. If that is what is affecting him, he can go hang. Nonsense! I wish you people could stay out of my way," She sighed heavily. I was shock-stricken by her position. My heart was broken to an extent whereby I felt as if the top floors of the flat I lodged had crumpled on me. I failed to get an appropriate response

She continued, "What's all your worry about disposing the cattle when they multiplied from the first two? Those two which will be left will still multiple anyway. I am disappointed by how you take your father's side. I am supposed to be taken care of and spoilt by my children like other parents are experiencing, but none of you ever does so, yet it is my right as a parent. Some parents are flying all over the world on trips sponsored by their lovely children and some of their children even compete to show their love, but as for me, I don't get even a sweet. Why do my own kids treat me like a barren woman? Most congregants put on new clothes throughout for half a year, but as for me, it's the same clothes every church day. Some of them are driving luxurious and expensive cars, and they splash mud on me as they drive past whilst I'm walking to and from church. All of you my children, you mean you can't even afford a wheelbarrow which may be handy to carry me to the main road to board a lift to hospital when I fall very sick? All parents need the attention of their children, who doesn't want it? Anyway, whom can I share this grievance, orphaned as I am? I bet, once I die, all of you will be in for it because of the way you are neglecting me. As for you, I have suffered a lot for your sake. I

16

sent you to boarding school and spent my paltry funds in the view that you would take care of me, but it was a mere waste of money. Had I spent that on my air tickets the better. I sent you to university to study, and you brought about that silly wife of yours who was sick-and-tired of mischief. Instead of studying and fulfilling the purpose of going to university, that men-monger fooled you into a marriage of convenience. Therefore, as I make my plans, I don't want anybody to stand in my way. Do you understand me! I don't like what you have done, and it must cease forthwith from today onwards." Mom complained. She cut off the line.

"Mom! Mom! Mom are you there?" I flip flopped my cellphone to check if the network was still connected. I tried to call once again, but her phone was switched off.

DREAMS OLD WOMEN HAVE

Yeukai 'Mimyie' Benhura

When I walked into room 99, I was greeted by a putrid stench that dizzied me for a moment. I could hear her simultaneously chewing loudly and farting. The curtains were drawn and the room was as dark as night. I could barely see her as she lay on the bed. I walked straight towards the windows and pulled open the curtains and windows in a fury.

She squealed in agony as the light blinded her and I had to supress a smile. I had just won my first victory. I turned back and studied her for a moment. She was lying on the ruffled bed, partly covered by the blankets, and her small frame was almost swallowed by the bed. She wore a pale peach bathrobe and a colourful headscarf. Her head rested on one arm and the other was placed on her hip. The arm looked bony and dry but there was a queer elegance to her pose.

She paid no heed to me, and slowly kept chewing some tree bark. Saliva mixed with the bark drooled from the corners of her mouth and she did not bother to wipe it off. When she finished chewing, she spat the remains on the floor. It was brown with a hint of green. She wiped her mouth with an upturned hand, cleaned off the residue and tidied her hand on her pink bed cover. If I had been less determined I would have quit in that moment.

"My name is Anita. What is yours?" I knew what her name was, but I had to gain control from the beginning. She looked up at me and scoffed, it was a long ten seconds before she answered.

"Suga!" she spat out as if it were rancid on her tongue.

"Now, Suga, I will be your aide for this month and, unlike the others, I will not tolerate any misbehaviour from you. Do we understand each other?"

18

She shrugged again, rose to sit up in her bed and began fluffing it, ignoring me.

"While I appreciate the implied meaning of your little act just now, I expect you to verbalise all communication. You are not a child so do not act as one. Understood?"

She gave me a cold stare, gritted what was left of her teeth and growled a 'yes' in response.

"Excellent." I began to tidy up her room, by picking up clothes strewn all over the floor, folding them neatly and packing them back into her closet.

"I have heard about you," I said, as I brought order to the room. I spoke about what I had heard about her and on occasion witnessed. I wanted her to know that I was not intimidated by her, but honestly I was. "You have terrorised everyone you have encountered in this institution since you arrived. There is no other resident as hated as you. The director was forced to make you a shared burden after you had harassed all your assigned aides. No one wants to take care of you, Suga, because somehow you feel it is okay to misbehave, insult and harass us. We even voted to have you chased out of the centre."

She clucked, almost as if she would be happy to be chased out of the centre.

Mama Suga,
She is a troubled soul,
A fiend walking among the living.
Tormenting all who cross her path,
Showing no remorse for her deeds.

"I will not let you torment me," I continued, "because I need this job. Mama Suga, you are not the only one haunted by the losses of the past. My father abandoned my mother when I was six, and she raised us alone. My brother, Amos Hanga, the big singer, I am sure you have heard his songs on the radio, left us when I was eighteen and never looked back. In the same year my brother Amos left, Mama had an accident that left her crippled. I need this job, Suga. I am all my family has."

I had no idea why I was telling her all my problems, but she needed to know what her actions would reap.

She began cleaning her fingernails, as if I was not in the room.

Not wanting to seem vulnerable,
She becomes a minx.
Her naughtiness is worse than that of a child,
She plays pranks on her aides,
Hurls profanities at anyone close enough to hear.

'Do you remember Siki? The aide you had last month. You traumatised her so much that she quit her job. If I remember correctly she said, you told her, 'Bring your man to me and I will show him what a real woman looks like.' Do you have any idea how much you hurt that poor woman?" I looked at her, waiting for her response, but she shrugged and began biting her nails and spitting them in my direction. My palm itched and I stopped myself from reaching out to slap her.

"Suga, that poor woman was having problems with her husband, which I am sure you and the rest of the centre know about. In less than a week after her husband's mistress came here and caused a scene, you decided to humiliate her like that? Did life not teach you to protect your sisters? You are a cruel woman, Suga." I hoped for some remorse

20

but she giggled. She clearly was not bothered by what I was saying, but I would continue. I was bound to hit a nerve soon enough.

Our silence was broken by a loud rap on the door that drew my attention away from her. The knock was followed by Tendai's popping her head in, but she quickly retreated. I had no option but to follow her outside to hear what she wanted.

Be wary as you change her bed pan,
She will crank herself up and release a fart that will stink up the whole ward.
We should stop feeding her those boiled eggs!
Sometimes she is a true bad hat,
Purposely humiliating any who dare come close,
And pour her bed pan urine on them.

I did not bother to excuse myself from mama Suga, I just dashed out of the room. I found Tendai standing with arms akimbo and frowning next to Natsai, who was busy texting. I figured why they had come.

"If you guys are here to warn me about mama Suga," I said, "I already know about her well enough. There is no need for you to worry about me, I will survive my time with her. It is just a month after all."

"Why did you not ask Thomas to excuse you from taking up the duty? He has the authority to go against the stupid coin toss. You know what she did to me, how can you go ahead with it?" Tendai's voice was high pitched and squeaky when she was agitated. Natsai had raised her head from her phone and was laughing, only because she had not yet faced Mama Suga.

"Who can forget what happened to you, Tendai? If you had not let her see that you were afraid she would have never done anything. So far you are the only one on whom she has poured urine. Thank God

21

for Thomas, you would have never survived day two with her, that I am sure of." Natsai was laughing loudly that the other residents began complaining in their rooms.

"Natsai, quiet! Tendai, I am glad that Thomas assisted you when you were put through the wringer, but I refuse to use my boyfriend's authority to make my life easier." With that, Tendai just shrugged and walked away.

"You know how she was treated by the old witch that is why she is so aggressive. You are the sweetest of us three that is why she is so overprotective of you. Talk to Thomas he will get you out of the duty. You are not strong enough to handle the drama. We are saying this because we care about you, just think about it dear." With that, Natsai also walked away, and left me wondering what I was trying to prove by going head to head with the most hated old woman at the centre.

"Was that the little mouse who liked to bath in my urine?" She asked as I walked in. I gave her a cold stare which only enticed her to attack even more.

"She even smiled when she had a taste of it, licked her lips even. That one was a good sport. She cried easily and lost her temper often. I like them irritable and wild and she was just perfect. If it was not for Mr Thomas who came to talk to me after she threatened to quit, I would have had more fun." She sounded pleased with herself.

"Will you shut up!" I screamed before I could stop myself.

"Oh, so you are like her."

I had two options, either to continue with my tantrum or to speak in a calmer tone but either way I was under her control and she was winning. I decided not to argue and carried on with folding her clothes.

She also fell silent.

Moments later she hoisted herself up from the bed groaning from the pains that ailed her, and I was almost tempted to run and assist her but I refrained from doing so. I was not going to show the fiend mercy. She dragged her feet across to the window, sat on her chair and stared outside with her back to me.

"So they are letting you marry that white boy of yours?" She asked when she was settled in her chair. Her voice was almost a whisper, like she was expressing an inner thought.

On the good days you see her staring out the window,
Dreaming of a life she lost,
But accepting comfort in having survived the losses.
Only her lips hint at rare moments of joy

It took me a moment to digest her question, yet I still did not realise her meaning. I looked at her reflection in the mirror, she looked in agony and strain like she had something weighing down on her soul. I was tempted to feel sorry for her, to actually directly blame myself for her meanness for whatever happened in her past.

"What did you say, Suga?" I asked her with a slight, and unintentional softness in my voice, which I regretted immediately.

"I asked why they will let you marry that white boy, Thomas, when they would not let me marry my Johnny."

The question shocked me because I had never thought of him as a white man. Just as a man. Then I quickly also realised Suga's meaning. She had taken an active role in the Second Chimurenga, the liberation struggle against the colonisers and during her time, interracial marriages were taboo. I wondered how she had failed to see that things had changed since independence. I was also curious to know who this Johnny was, but I was sure if I asked she would shut down.

I walked over to her bed and began to put fresh linen on it without responding to her question. She did not say anything but instead moaned and from the corner of my eye I saw her wipe tears off quickly. Or maybe she needed a little encouragement. I still had my reservations about being kind to her after she had harassed everyone else.

"Mama Suga, what happened with your Johnny?" I spoke softly.

She sat in silence tears streaming down her parched cheeks. She let them flow freely without a single sob. I let her mourn her past, she had clearly lost so much and had held in the pain for too long.

The voices from the past haunt her,
Her fist clenches and you know the wailing has begun.
She mourns for her life past,
A life filled with regret and shame.

"They came and took us from home when I was fifteen. Already at that time I had left school because no one wanted an educated wife and also the times were hard for my family. When they came I was excited to be a part of the heroes that sacrificed their lives for our country, I never knew in what way I was expected to sacrifice my life." She cleared her throat and I rushed to get her some water.

"We were taken to the base, and taught how to use guns, grenades and knives for close combat. This training lasted a few weeks, then one night Comrade Singer came and woke a few of us, loaded us into a truck and we were taken to the capital city, Salisbury. It was a long, silent drive, because we realised what part in the war we were about to play." She stopped and looked out the window.

She gently caressed her face as if she were reading a message imprinted on the wrinkles on her face. She placed her left fingers on her lips and began sobbing softly. The woman had a lot of hurt hidden within, and my relationship with Thomas must have caused some release. It was hard to hate her now. I was filled with curiosity and sympathy for her.

She yearns the memories lost,
Her eyes squinted in search for a better view.
She yearns for the beautiful views ages gone.
Her lips pursed longing long for the kiss only life gave,
What those lips have tasted, only they can testify!

"The comrades had selected the few beautiful ones of us to act as spies. It was well known that some of the white soldiers had acquired a liking for the black girls, so we were used to gain information from these soldiers. We went through training on how to be prostitutes, cleaners, laundry maids and baby sitters in targeted areas. I was placed as a cleaner in Major Luke Robertson's house. My job was to clean while I eavesdropped on all conversations that were made concerning the war." All this while she had spoken with her back to me. Now, she stood up and reached out her hand to ask for assistance.

I noticed a tiny gold ring that had what looked like an emerald stone on her ring finger. Spending time with Thomas I had become acquainted with fine jewellery. I wondered if this Johnny had given it to her.

"You wonder if it's the real thing," she chuckled. "It is very real. My Johnny gave it to me when he proposed. I had been in Major Robertson's employment for about six months when his handsome son Johnny arrived from England where he had been attending university. I will never forget the day I met him because that is the day I began to live." She giggled like a teenager in love, I knew how she must have felt because I felt the same way about Thomas.

Her back arched,
With old age and toils of her youth.
Her hands roughened,
Tremble as she reaches to feel the wrinkles on her once beautiful face.
She must have caused quite the stir in her day.

"I was treated like a slave by the Major and his household, and this hardly changed with the arrival of Johnny. He was the only one who showed me any sympathy. He often saw his mother abuse me and he would come to comfort me in private. We were innocent and chaste in our love that remained undeclared for the longest while. On my days off, I would go and report any news I had and afterwards I would meet him at a cottage owned by one of his friends' family. They were more sympathetic to the black man's plight." She smiled so sweetly. I knew the memories were wonderful.

"You have never known a love more beautiful than forbidden love. We flourished in our love, sneaking behind his family and my superiors. We were on opposite sides of the war and we had no right to be so. On the day he proposed, I had been beaten with a wooden spoon on my back at his mother's orders. The whole household heard my screams and he had saved me. In that moment, I knew he loved me. He fought with his parents about the insubordination and suddenly proposed to me before his parents and the staff. Of course I said yes, even though I knew we were both being silly. The other staff all clapped their hands in excitement and his mother slapped me straight across the face. I had expected some form of resistance but not a slap. From that moment, it all became chaotic." I felt her heartbreak.

Some days she has nightmares.
She wakes up screaming and drenched in sweat,

Lost in her previous life.

"That moment is the source of all the nightmares I get at night. I knew they did not like me because of my skin colour, my position in society, but I never knew anyone could be capable of such hatred for another human being. I never chose to be as I was and neither did Johnny, we were merely victims of God's creation, that he made in his own image. How cruelly dissimilar his image is."

She mutters under her breath,
When she does not get her way
Mischief and pain are an artwork that nature painted on her face

"His mother dragged me out of the house by my apron and skirts. She shouted vulgarities at me, his father stood there and watched. Jonny screamed at his mother to stop and his father punched him in the face. She demanded the ring, I refused to part with it, ran from the house, and headed to the base. There, I found the commander waiting for me and he paraded me as a traitor. The comrades took turns kicking and punching me until I passed out. When I woke up, I was lying in a forest in Mount Selinda with broken ribs and swollen eyes. From that moment I knew I had to hide from the comrades all my life because if they found out I was still alive, they would kill me."

"Is that why you fought so hard not to be taken in by the guards the day they found you?"

"Yes, it has become so hard for me to trust even the people of my own kind. I fear for my life and I have no idea why I just shared my story with you." She looked so vulnerable that I could see all the pain she had been carrying all her life melt away.

"Do you know what happened to your Johnny, Mama? Did you ever find him?"

"No. I never dared to go back and look for him. He was lost to me from that day. I still love him even after all these years. I got a job as a house maid at a farm just outside Harare, owned by a white couple. With the new government, their farm was taken and they left for England. I was left homeless and jobless. I then moved to Harare and moved from one maid job to another until I was too old to be employed. I never saw my family and never married because I was waiting for my Johnny."

"Maybe we can look for him, Mama. Would you like that?" She nodded in response and I went to sit by her as we spoke of her Johnny and my plans to find him.

THE BLACK CAT

Phumulani Chipandambira

We sadly woke up, our feet nibbled. Simba was very angry and he suggested that we must kill the black fat cat.

Rats had feasted on us that previous night. Rats do not easily fall into traps.

"He is too lazy," Simba shouted "Hitler deserves death!"

Papa named it Hitler because of its whiskers and brown eyes. Hitler was one of its kind. 1 hate cats but Papa likes them. He loves pets, he always let Shumba, the dog, eat the left-overs from his china plate. Mama complained about it but Papa never listened.

We looked for it in all places, we searched in the bedroom, inside the shack that we use as the kitchen, in the pit latrine, we searched everywhere, but we could not locate it.

It was still early for it to wander into the neighbourhood, the sun had risen, its rays licking the Katanga township, making our shadows appear too long. Mama had risen early and went out, when we were still asleep.

We knew she would not come back till noon. She is a hawker, she sells floor polish and brooms every morning. Papa did not sleep at home once again, he was out on one of his numerous beer drinking errands.

It took us two hours to find it. We found it sleeping under the shade of the green banana tree leaves, relaxed. Hitler had a shinning black fur, it walked with feline grace. It also refused to eat dirty and raw things. It was very different from the mangy cats that stay at the dumpsite.

"Let us starve it before we hang it," I suggested.

"Oh no lets sell it," Simba shouted.

"Nobody buys a black cat. What if we dump it at the shops," I suggested.

Simba knew that l was afraid of killing it. He teased me many times, saying that I cannot even kill a cockroach and he called me a coward of the cowards.

Dumping a cat was not also easier. We had to put it in a sack, tie it at the top and walk without turning back. We would then leave the sack in the forest or at the crossroads.

"Oh, no! Let's kill it!" Simba brushed my idea aside.

Hitler looked at us with its big brown eyes as big as Mama's raincoat buttons. Simba patted it softly on its back, grabbed it on the neck and quickly shoved it under the upturned metal dish. l wondered what was he up to. He sat on top of the dish and the cat mewed and scratched the insides of the dish.

"Do you want to suffocate it?" l asked and he said "No, come and sit here."

My mind was puzzled and I thought he wanted to kill it by knifing it at the throat like what Mama always do when slaughtering the chickens.

He fetched a stone and two big sticks and I waited pondering what if he was possessed and being tormented by the unrelenting demons. He drummed the dish once and the cat that had relaxed began to scratch the insides of a metal dish, it was a futile attempt to free itself for the dish was too big. It was a big dish that l could not lift on my own.

"Lets sing and dance " Simba shouted. "Sing Nyasha ! Sing, I shot the Sherif" he cried. Bob Marley is Papa's best musician, he once said his music heals the poor man's soul.

30

"Simba please, lets leave it alone" I was no longer interested in his games.

"Come on Nyasha, be a man," he drummed to the tune of reggae and what I could do was to jump up and down. I could not shake my waist. Papa sometimes danced like that, he had started to keep long hair. Neighbours teased us by calling to us "Rasta-children".

He drummed the upturned dish for so long. l stopped dancing when l felt tired. "Simba that's enough", I shouted. Simba stubbornly remained sitted and continued on drumming the metal dish. He then stood up from the metal dish and followed me onto the streets to play with other boys.

We played the ball of rags and we forgot about Hitler, our black cat that wore a purple ribbon around its neck.

We later learnt that it was a taboo to kill a black cat- *felicide*. A cat dies thousands time before its actual death.

When we returned to our house, I lifted the dish and the cat fled blindly. It hit the fence, picked itself and ran along the street before it disappeared around the bend.

Simba fell down with laughter.

Since that day we never saw it again. It never returned. Those who saw it running said that it looked like a black veldt hare.

When Mama came back home from her routines, she was very tired of walking. "Did you two feed Hitler and Shumba with yesterday's left-overs?" she aske.

"Yes, Mama" Simba lied!

We took the plates and dishes to the sink and we began to eat the left-overs. *Makoko!*

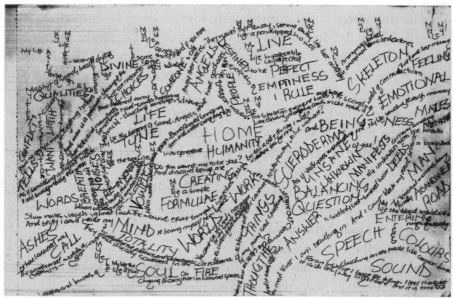

My Life

Artwork © by Tendai R Mwanaka

GHOSTLY GALLEON

John Eppel

A ghostly galleon plies the seas
that give and take, build and break
on Africa's ex-colonies:
on Mozambique, Namibia,
(sometimes mild and sometimes wild),
Angola and South Africa.

Bang, bang, bang, the An Yue Jiang
is looking for a port,
but workers on the Durban docks
said, "Nothing of the sort!

"Take your AKs somewhere else,
your mortars and grenades;
they'll use those bullets on working folk,
boys with dreadlocks and girls with braids,
waiters, vendors, gardeners, maids,
labourers with picks and spades,
farmers dragging the oxen's yoke."

There is a ghostly galleon
that plies the southern seas;
it carries death for working folk:
cannons and RPGs.

It tried to dock in Durban
to drop its deadly load,

but the Durban Dockers' Union
upheld the workers' code.

Well it's a bang, bang, bang, the An Yue Jiang
Is sailing round the Cape
with toys for the Boys that make a loud noise,
that kill and maim and rape.

Salute the Durban Dockers
salute those workers bold:
they saved a thousand comrades
from misery untold.
They saved a thousand comrades,
but only for a day:
the ghostly galleon will be back —
terror is here to stay.

PUNGWE

John Eppel
[Matobo, 1984]

Masoja were speaking in Shona, their sticks
were mopane - that wood is like iron;
broke all my arms and this leg that can't bend;
yes, fan belts, umfo, and kicking with boots;
made us undress and do sex with a goat;
then with our bums; sang: "PasiLoNkomo."
But first they khetha some youngsters, not me,
was my brother, my cousin, my neighbours...
on one side putting three, other side three;
then they give me a pick and a fotshol,
say dig, and I dig; on this side one grave,
other side one, not deep, to end of my
thing; yes, naked in front of our mothers,
our sisters; gebha as deep as the end
of your thing: mbolo. Made them to kneel
by the side of the graves; shooting them dead.
We were dancing and singing, and screaming
with pain; they beat us and kicked us for hours,
umfo; yes, calling us dissidents
whilest we sang: "PambiliLoMugabe.

SONG FOR WOZA*

John Eppel

Women of this land arise,
fling your windows open wide,
let the breeze of change, denied,
let it take you by surprise.
Amandlaomama!

Let it take you to the streets,
walk for freedom, walk for peace,
disarm with charm the armed police,
give them flowers and home-made treats.
Amandlaabafazi!

Let it blow through corridors
where men of power strap their boots,
sip hot liquor, smoke cheroots,
boast of virgins and of whores.
Amandlaamankazana!

Let it, when you go to jail,
keep your foreheads cool, your hearts,
keep refreshed the gentler arts —
then let it grow into a gale.
Amandlaisifazana!

*Women Of Zimbabwe Arise - courageous activists, forever being imprisoned

These streets

John J.J Dongo

Dust filled dream laden
Where boys play and girls play, live out dreams
Where the sounds of laughter and joy can be heard from over yonder
Take me to the streets from whence I came from
The umbilical cord that is mine planted in the earth
I hear it calling
Take me to the streets where I bruised knees and scraped legs
Our bittersweet relationship
But the love I had for it saw me next morning
Running up in the glare of the morning sun
With band aids that represented battles bruises
But ultimately showed my loyalty
Take me to the streets where my first fight taught me not to run
But graced me with honor in defeat
Take me to the streets where I saw many a broken dream
As we transcended from the joyful bliss of childhood
To the responsibilities of life
Take me to the streets where I traded in freedom
For the bondage of a nine to five
These are the streets that made me
The ghetto raised me
Birthed me with dreams and disappointment
Take me back to the streets to make testament
To the new generation
These streets are with you, not of you, but in you
Take me back to the streets
We shall make it known, dreamers should dreams

And dreams shall be lived

You are Beautiful
Lisa Jaison

I knew it from the first time your seed sprouted
The quintessential evidence of when God remembers
On his time, by his will and his grace – that's you
Evoking all the things higher beings only yearn for
Perfect

Taking the world's eyes off the pain, to focus on the majesty of the
miracle of you
Creating a reason and purpose for life by just being
The embodiment of hope, forgiveness, passion and will,
I marvel in awe, love, compassion, humility
Stunned

A whirlwind of innocence, second chances and rewritten destiny
I bet the creator chuckles in satisfaction at the job perfectly executed
that you are
The signal of his greater purpose and desire
The mark of his will
Seamless

For you, the sun yearns to shine brighter
Flowers overarch to blossom more radiant
Dreams are motivated into visions and manifested reality
You are the sun that breaks through the African summer storm

Beautiful

I dare to proclaim no women ever bore a son as perfect as you
Been so abundantly consecrated or indulged
A classic case when God played favorites to your parentage
The overwhelming abundance of a mother's love
That's me, to hell and back for only you, my son

THE ORACLE OF A ZAIN

Andrew Huje

Did they ask you who I was?
Tell them I'm a brazen-faced zain
Left to gobble of their mildew ridden bread,
Left broken in the tempest,
A stooge drowning in soot,
I am the abandoned soul
Waiting for abatement.
I am mobbed up in this blackness,
Strangled in this inferiority-
Yet my prowess carried you
Into a state you abode
Basking in luxury,
Revering your pinkish colour
You regard as white.
I'm the zain rendered dull,
Powerless, devoid of good.
I am the black poet,
I am Africa, the dark continent-
Unappreciated yet I cradle wealth
You milk away. I'm shaken by your ignorance.
Brutalized.

DOLL'S HOUSE

Andrew Huje

Father today child tomorrow,
Kings crawl where mongrels did;
Dark now tomorrow shine,
Cooking in a dirty pot, a play,
An allusion, just stupidity they say;
How demons are birthed from childplay we know not;
Smile child it's just a foreplay,
These demons are not demons,
Just your brothers pretending;
But how come in dreams and fears?
How in shadows I feel a cold,
In dances I lose movement?
In tears I smile. Pain protects and fear does,
So fear not child,
It's foreplay, just kidding;
Your brothers and sisters are playing.

HOLD ON
Anesu Nyakubaya

In the loneliest of nights
And the darkest of days,
When your pump of life
Yearns and longs,
When it reaches out
On its tippy toes, longing
And when all that is visible
Is nothing but darkness,
When all hope is lost
And your soul has given up on the Lord
And grief is the only blanket you identify with,
When you start listening
To the little voices in your head,
Articulating your unsound innermost
And making a mockery of every dream you ever dreamt of achieving
When their chants become a mantra
That instead building you breaks you
When you reach the edge
Of your 2D, flat surfaced reality
And life is just a dark void
An abyss
When you get there, hold on a little longer
I am here, I am coming for you
To hold your hand and bring you back to light
Back to manicured gardens with picket fences, and rose beds
To bliss
I got you

Hold on, I am coming
Hold on and know I am here

FAREWELL (DEDICATED TO RAE LYRIC)
Anesu Nyakubaya

The sun has folded
Giving way to the moon
That it may enjoy your beauty
And be serenaded by your voice

He has asked you to pass on the kisses
He so earnestly placed on your skin
To his love on the other side
He could not hold on to you

His selfless love for the moon
Has sanctioned
Gifted her you, his most precious
He has taken a bow, to the love of his life
That she may breathe
And be brought to life by the creativity that juices your veins
Go well She of the Sun
Go and bless the moon and its children,
the same way you bless the sun and day walkers alike

HAKUNA MATATA

Mandla Mavolwane

A soothing anthem is audible
Its lyrics bear a touch of bliss.
The descendants of the motherland inherited it.
But does their state qualify them to dance
To this harmonius melody.

Existing amongst human beasts
The feminine struggle for equality
Rebuked and violated to never again rise.
Who said they do not possess the prowess
Of mastering politics and science?
Who said they are mere child bearers?

We dream of building a future
A future with a touch of tranquillity,
Zero discrimination and absolute equality.
How can you build a future without true nurturers
Who will make sure the future is hate free?

The motherland is a land of serenity
Serenity that composed hakuna matata
"There are no worries for the rest of your days"
The chain of no worries oxidized
As the sound of the ancient anthem
Is an insult to the opprssed caregivers.

Hakuna Matata is slowly fading away.

A huge task lay at hand
A task to give meaning to the renowned African anthem.
Let us bring back the days
When everyone sang it from the heart.
Everyone including the smothered women
As we long to hear angelic voices
Confidently vocalize Hakuna Matata

Fare-thee-well

Bruno Shora

(In memory of a Constable and all the victims of a heretical religious ideology, Nov 2012)

A somber atmosphere hovers around the small town,
As a dark nimbus cloud loosely hangs in the stratosphere,
Civilians, the military and the clergy converge,
Not during a civil unrest,
Not for a pass out parade,
But to fare-the-well,
The Constable,
Who has unceremoniously and untimely departed,
Not for any diplomatic mission or assignment in Kosovo,
Not at the battle front,
Not during the course of executing her duties,
But through some tragic, un-orthodox practices,
In the hands of wolves in sheep skin,
In the hands of self styled mid-wives,

Birds of the air are asked to observe some moments of silent,
As a gentle wind blows, only good enough to keep furthers afloat,
A deem sunlight illuminates the cemetery,
Civilians' hats are off,
As the Police Orchestra classically plays the ravioli,
The trumpeteering, piercing, melodious tune seem to be uniting all,
        the living and the dead,
The casket   hesitantly, reluctantly, gently subsides,
6 feet beneath the sea level,
The rest of the officers here present temporarily suffer a minor stroke,

The firing party makes some gunshots into the atmosphere,
The gun firing is quickly diffused by ululations from the amazed crowed which is
      part of the send-off,
The gun-salute briefly reminds senior citizens here present
      of the historic 1966 Battle of Chinhoyi and the 2nd Chimurenga,
Shovels are on standby,
"Soil to soil",
The Chaplain and pastors seem to be agreeing
Oh no, there she goes,
Never to return, in this life,

Your efforts are commendable,
For nine months you endured the agony,
The agony of carrying within you,
An alien,
A flower,
A flower that never was,
With the hope of seeing it blossom,
Life then left you,
When you were trying to give life,
The flower could also not help it, it also withered,
 Not this way Edith,
Not in a forest,
Not in a tent,
Where survival is a matter of chance,
Shall we call it a death ward or camp?
Had you left behind an exhibit,
Our hearts would not be bleeding this way,
They could neither save you nor the infant,

Neither do they possess the pre-requisites of mid-wifely,
Later on the facilities and the equipment,
Let the earthily and heavenly courts seat and convict them,

     before showing them the doors of mercy,
Convict them for negligently causing the demise of many,
Many of whom they have brainwashed and blinded,
Many of whom they have denied access to the hospital,
Many of whom they have denied access to proper health attention,
Many of whom they have denied access to contraceptives and antenatal
care,
Many of whom they have denied access to education,
Many of whom they have denied access to economic empowerment,
Many of whom they have denied access to freedom of worship,
Many of whom they have denied access to the truth,
Many of whom they have prematurely forced into
     polygamous marriages and the risks therein,
All this in the name of the spirit,
Who taught them this?
Could it be the Lord?
Could it be the Spirit?
Could it be the word?
Certainly it's not the Lord, the Spirit and the Word I know,
but what is wrong with modernism if it is there to make
     human life better in one way or the other?

To you Constable,
And all the victims,
Of primitive, barbaric bondage,
Only if you knew,

Only if you could flee with your lives,
You would have done something,
You shall always be remembered.

MUFAKOSE!

Chenjerai Mhondera

Mufakose;
Pamweya wakafa,
Panyama wafazve!
Uyu ndiwo Mufakose!

Uku uri kutsva,
Uku wakarumwa.
Uyu ndiwo Mufakose.
Wangove mufakose!

Uku uri kurohwa,
Uku uri kunzi nyarara!
Wangove Mufakose.

Uku uri musungwa,
Uku uri kunzi ukareva wawedzera usungwa.
Wangove Mufakose!
Ruwa rwose- Mufakose!

Kuti uku wonzi gara,
Uku wonzi wakagarirei?
Wangove Mufakose!

Ruwa rwose- Mufakose!

Kuti woita chironda,
Uku nhunzi dzokudya;
Wangove Mufakose!
Kwese kwese, Mufakose!

Kuti wokunda musarudzo,
Wokundazve kusatonga!
Ndiwo Mufakose!
Nyika yose Mufakose!

Kuti wako mudiwa oti ndipe ndisakusiye,
Womupa okusiya;
Ndiwo Mufakose!
Murudo, Mufakose.

Kuti wopa mudiwa wako pfugama udye,
Adya, waguta oti hauna kumbondipa ini!
Uyu ndiwo Mufakose!
Haiwa, Mufakose!

Kuti nditaure Mufakose,
Kuti ndinyararezve Mufakose!
Haiwa, Mufakose!
Wangove Mufakose!

DOUBLE DEATH!

Chenjerai Mhondera
Translation from Shona by Chenjerai Mhondera

Double death;
Spiritually dead,
Physically dead.
Such is double death!

From one end, burning.
The other bitten!
Such is double death,
And that is double death!

On one end, you are beaten;
The other, shut up!
Such is double death.

You are the accused,
And to speak out you are warned;
Whatever you say shall be used
Against you in court of law!
Such is double death!
A whole location- Mufakose!

Someone says wait here!
Another says, what are you waiting for?
Such is double death!
A whole location- Mufakose!

You've got wounded,
And flies keep the wound from not healing.
Such is double death.
Everywhere, double death!

You win elections after all difficulties,
And still you succeed not to rule!
That is double death.
The whole society, suffer continue!

Your lover demands it from you,
To bribe them not abandon you.
You give,
And dumps you;
That's double death!
In love, double death.

You give self wholly to your lover,
And say, bend and enjoy!
After session, you are full;
He denies responsibility!
Such is double death!
Oh shame, it's double death!

If I speak, it's double death.
If again, I keep silent, it's suffer continue!
Oh so it's double death!
Surely, it is suffer continue!

Mufakose- Double death/Suffer continue/location, Mufakose.

THE TRUTH OF MY BLACKNESS

Chido J Ndoro

We've been sitting here
By the outside
Waiting for the mans to come out
The big mans who sit in their meetings
Who think for us
And tell us what they have thunk
The heat has been burning us
The rain has rained us
And they still sit and thinks
We have waited for so long
For them to tells us what to do
Do we gets to get into the house or no?
I don't think they wants us in there
Because very long ago
My father tried to got in
But they kicksed him out
Naked and died
They sayed the dogs had mistaked him for a monkey
When are we gets into the bigs house
Because we can't reads anymore
We can't writes
We just sit and waited
Our teachers were builded
A little shades
But it was rained on by the ice rain

So now they are being burned and rained on
And they still sits and thinks
Now its getting worser
They turn off the outside lights
At the evening
When we couldn't see nothing
But we can see the inside lights on
We cannot hear them speaks
Because they speak in shutted up voices
Mother sayed they talks about us
But what about us i asks
She sayes they dont wants us to ate the cake
What is a cake, i wonders
And why is it eated?
Why do i have to runs all the mornings?
Why do i have to revenge father?
I dont wants to runs and fought
I wants to sleeps under the tree
And curled under my newspapers blankets
Mother, why do you speak of freedomlessness
We are freedomful
Can't you see?
We sell anything
We sells anywheres we want
They never gets out of the thinking house
And we never get out
Of the sun, winter, windy, rains
We are always in theres
And they are thinking all the times
But mother i have heared you talks

Of some days and some nights
When they would come out and tell what they have thunk
And they bring out the cake
For you to see
But you never eated it
How do you know it is tasteful when you have not eated it mother?
How do you know if i runs all the mornings
The dogs will tired of running for me?
How do you know foughting for the cake
Is why we are live?
What if i dies like father?
What if dogs mistakes me for monkey too?
We are freedomful mother
The cake i have not eated
Is no appetite for me
If we are freedomless
Maybe you should fought for us
Because its unpossible
For me to fighted for what i have not saw.

ZVIKUKUTU
Simbarashe Chirikure

Rinoda kuwirirana
Rigoda gadziriro yakakwana
Richida kubudirana pachena
Rigodazve kuenzanisa.

Chabatwa nerwerudyi, rweruboshwe ngarwuchibatewo.
Patsikwa nereruboshwe, rerudyi rotopatsikawo.
Mukunaka nekuipa kwazvo,
Iwe fanana nezuva risingashanduke.

Kurigonera wotosimba senjanji
Unofanira kumira wakati twi-i semupuranga
Kungorereka chete waigochera pautsi
Pakuita kazevezeve wadyara ruvengo
Barika rinoda kugona kwete kuvavarira sahwira wangu.

Tough

Simbarashe Chirikure
Translated from Shona into English by Oscar Gwiriri

Fairness and friendliness is game
You ought to prepare for it
Transparency is the answer
You've to be open and diligent.

What the right hand knows
The left hand must know.
A well coordinated step is best,
In good times and hard times,
Be still like the sun's stature.

You ought to be rail steel strong,
Straight forward and accountable.
A slip is as good as a down fall,
Favouritism sows seeds of hatred.
Polygamy isn't for the faint hearted.

MURAMBATSVINA

Oliver Mtapuri

Anogeza
Anopoda
Anodyaega
Murambatsvina

Vamwe vanoti zvikwereti zvega zvega
Vachiti 'Zvakanakatinozvidawo'
Anobwinya
Anonyemwerera
Anosekerera
NdiMurambatsvinauyo

Gwama rake rakazaranemari
Shamwari anadzo
Hadzipere
Mambakwedza ndeake
Masikati ndeake
Manheru ndeake
Anoitwa Murambatsvina

Igotwe rekwani irori?
Uno abvunza uno
Hapana anoziva
Mazino ake akachena kuti ngwee
NdiMurambatsina iyeye

Ukabwaira, anotora achinyemwerera

Aneshangu dzakatsvinda
Asi imbavha, gororo rekupedzesera
Iwe Murambatsvina ibvapano.

The-One-who-refuses-to-be-dirty
Oliver Mtapuri

He dresses well
Always cosmeticised
He eats alone
The-One-who-refuses-to-be-dirty

Others say it is all borrowed money and time
Saying 'We also love the good things and goodies'
Sparkling
Always smiling
Infectious smiles
There you are, the-One-who-refuses-to-be-dirty

Wallet overflowing with money
He has friends galore
So many
The dawn seemingly belongs to him
The afternoons are his
The nights are his
His name is, the-One-who-refuses-to-be-dirty

Whose last born is this?
You ask everyone

No one knows
His teeth are glitteringly white
That is the-One-who-refuses-to-be-dirty

Swiftly
If you blink, he quickly snatches from you
Shiny shoes
He is a thief, inside out
You, the-One-who-refuses-to-be-dirty, go away and disappear into the
thin air

FLAMES WON'T CREATE FLAWS
Haile Saize I

The bruises of burns on her beautiful face
Are tattoos of championship
Certified marks of endurance
The foundation of overwhelming prowess
She is a heroine
A hope of the hopeless feminine
She bulldozed abuse
Her sympathetic attitude overcoming rejection
She's the reconciliation
Recreation
She deserves a crown of recognition
Reconstruction
She forgives
She teaches
Flames won't create flaws
She is human, why do you abuse her?

Chimurenga

Haile Saize I

Where are you Chimurenga?
Are you satisfied to abort Zimbabwe?
Plunk the children to cry
And wonder why you must die
Chimurenga* we thought you were with us
Both in agony and success
But only until we realized your plastic smile
Then you had to desert us
Left us vulnerable to internal power struggles
Yes you fought the invasions
European expansion
The colonialism
Imperialism and all the schisms
To leave us the divisions
The fight against the Shona* and Ndebele* ethnic groups
And the corruption
The vote; an imperial spot!
They are still rigging
Chimurenga please come stand with me
The Maji-maji where is your uprising?
Come confine the cowards into oblivion
And let Tanganyika* feel the haven of peace

~Chimurenga - a Shona word for war of liberation struggle.*
~Shona - Zimbabwean language or people*
~Ndebele -Zimbabwean minority language or its people*
~Tanganyika -former Tanzanian name*

Victims Are Once Beaten

Haile Saize I

It's sad for us blacks to say we are free
To say the war of freedom were fought
And that our elders died for it a couple of years
I mean the young and the old
Who fought much bold?
So tirelessly for this land and its people to be free
Songs of freedom were sang
Uhuru drums were played,
Echoed much audible than the bullets which pierced these innocent souls
Victims!
Our people; the black posse!
Heroes of our yester-years died to set Africans free
Free from tax
Slavery; cheap labour
Free from colonial economic slavers
Free from debts
But as these heroes died
Our freedom likewise was ate like bread
Leaving us vulnerable
Black politicians in their stupidity;
Foolish wisdom of making a foe his friend!
Converted our freedom into lip-reconciliation
Even turned into puppets
Of the so-called U.N- Untied Nations*
International Monetary Fraud*
And the White Bank*

Voices of freedom are stuck
Casted into oblivion
We thought we were done
But I can see
The victims are once more beaten!

~United Nations* -is the so-called United Nations for it's a hypocritical organization
~International Monetary Fraud* -is the IMF International Monetary Fund for it is a fraud
~White Bank* -the World Bank. For Africa is not part of the main agenda, which world is it without Africa

Broken
Jabulani Mzinyathi

Bearing the dead weight
The weight of emptiness
The ingratitude of a taker
One who is eternally insatiable

Thought it was built on reciprocation
Reality now delivers a back hander
That it all was just a soap bubble
Perhaps a mirage on the road

Like a leech the agony lingers
Shards of broken promises
Smithereens of those dreams
Echoes of betrayal bouncing

There is no hiding place
From the hailstorms of emotions
A dry barren wind blows
Maybe one day soon rain falls

Toita Tichiyeuchidzana

Jabulani Mzinyathi

Takazvireva mukati tinopenga
Takati ichi chingoma choririsa
Mukati imi izvi hazvina mugumo
Makakanganwa henyu kwazvakabva

Inonyika inavenevayo
Motamba henyu makachenjera
Musakanganwa chazuro nehope
Moita muchicheuka kwamakabva

Zvekukakanganwa kutiushe madzoro
Iyi inhaka yemusiiranwa musarivara
Mashoko aya akare moita muchiyeuka
Simba rehove ririmo mumvura

Hecho kochitsvambe ikoko kwamuri
Zvekuchapfanya zviya zvokupazadura
Zvavaenzi vanogarisa bodo, kwete
Iko kuzivanguva handiti kwakanaka

Lest we forget
Jabulani Mzinyathi

Branded us nutty cases
That the end was nigh we had said
That the bubble would burst we said
To you there was no end in sight

The owners lay claim to this country
Watch your back when having your fun
Reality will always deliver its back hander
Your roots do not ever forget

The reins must be handed over
The essence is that of an inheritance
Those timeless teachings of old remember
For a fish out of water meets its demise

The ball now is there in your court
Those gluttonous tendencies leave
No visitor should overstay his welcome
Time is the master always remember that

Clay feet giant

Jabulani Mzinyathi

The deification was complete
That myth of invincibility peddled
The guns turned against the people
Those that mattered not any more

But some of us did sound warnings
That those seemingly loyal hunting hounds
That those guns would turn, yes
Turn against the real enemy

The tanks rolled then into town
The guns then faced the real enemy
Detained in his own impregnable fortress
Detained in opulence and profligacy

The noose was tightening
It had happened before
The numerous trips to that Acre
The handiwork to tuck away

The sycophants had descended
Like flies into a pit latrine
Like hungry vultures to carrion
Then push came to shove

Retrospection

Learnmore Edwin Zvada

We used to dine at that small cafe just outside Chitungwiza
We had our favorite spot at the back
Two wooden chairs and a table with a wiggle
There was that waitress you fancied
Tiny waist, big eyes and a lulu smile
Every time she would serve us the one meal on the menu
Sadza, bathed in a pool of soup and some lean strips of chicken
And you almost didn't see the chicken till really dug in
And every Friday night it was like that

Then there were days along 1ˢᵗ Street
Peeping through the tall storefront displays of expensive furniture
shops
The endless debates on what would fit where in the derelict hovel we
rented in Unit B
A pack of maputi shuttling between our hands all the while
And it was you who would always finish it off…
(Of course, you wanted the nuts at the bottom of the packet)
I remember the stories we shared
The lewd jokes you always threw in-between
I always prognosticated the future
And you would take it all in to the last wordage
Like an overzealous schoolboy

Each time your girlfriend dumbed you, you would call
I would show up with a bottle of cheap whiskey
Ready to drown your sorrows six-shots under

Thereafter, I would listen to you curse on end
And we always agreed that this was a requisite immorality
Today, I play Russian roulette with the memories of you
Betting on the one that's bound to make me cry
I laugh at that; see, they are just old thoughts
Perhaps outstaying their welcome
But why do I feel the urge to cry at that?

I'm sitting in my car, stuck in Friday's traffic jam
There is a song issuing from the stereo
Toto's Hold the line
I recall how we used to 'chop' the lyrics
Yet we sang our hearts,
Whenever the old codger next door,
Played it on his acoustic gramophone
It hurts me now that all I am left with are the memories
And a dead stereo you left in my apartment
So I miss you dearly, painfully still
I wish you were around
So that I could tell you I found a girl to marry
Tiny waist, big eyes and that lulu smile
And that would be something to drink to
For old times' sake

Too Big A Noise For My Trade

Learnmore Edwin Zvada

I have not the lines to describe the whim of a
painter fashioning a portrait of a kept woman,
nor have I, for once, saddled my gaze upon the
seesawing bosom, supple skin's dimpled rise,
the rounds and turns of a damsel's posture
looming out of a steamy illustrator's zoomed lens

How unfortunate it is to be without the artistry to
describe such sinuous a summation of feminine
artwork, its rendered foreign to me, that adverse
ineptness straddling up on my tongue
needless to say, the portrait in itself is an object
of forlorn ambience to the eyes of the escapist,
the one extremist I am inescapably mutating into

It isn't surprising why my verses maintain that I
have tastes colder than a witch's ears, unwrapped
to such a cruel set of words, too soon I'm bound
to step aside and let the painter and his paint do
what they know best.

Poisoned

Michael White

Sweet was it on the palate.

Something of a balanced mixture and texture of elements whose chemistry, complex and perplexing. Stinging it was as it went up my temple than it did to my stomach.

Sweat droplets found their place on my forehead and immediately my senses began failing.

Slowly but effectively the poison found its way to my core. Sensations unaccountable overwhelmed me manifesting the inherent vices.

Severe convulsions soon followed, the eyes were failing and the last sight they captured were scattered capsules labeled jealous.

Victory

Moreblessing Size Tafireyi

I will not surrender
 to this savage dance of fire
this dance of pain
this dance of madness
this dance that wants to turn my pain and anger into an inferno.

My voice seems to be coming from the valley of doom
My pain makes me feel as though a stone has been dropped
with a splash into the still waters of my soul
I'm encircled by spreading waves
no end it seems to this river of fire.
This river of pain
this river of madness

They laugh in victory
they think she has fallen finally
Never! I declare with desert winds in my eyes.
With negation I shout out with all the power of earth and sky
my voice will not melt
I will rise like an eagle in the African sky

I will stop this time bomb tied to my life
the beauty within me has not died yet
my heart is still beautiful and unique like a pearl
my worth is above rubies.

Their tiny feet will not step on my dreams

their laughter no longer has the acid test of pain and hatred.
I will not be a statue of stone
I will fight for what's my mine.

I have found a haven in the depths of my soul
it has offered me protection.
All the beauty of my heart is exploding into a rainbow of joy, victory
and rhythm.
Rhythm that has an acoustic note
you cannot resist this beauty
this celebration of life
this my celebration of who I am.

When we meet

Moreblessing Size Tafireyi

When we meet /it won't be love at first sight
No sparks will fly in my eyes
But I will see the oceans and skies in yours
Your experiences will show me how they have flown and drowned.
In mine you will see a lost soul drifting between light and darkness
We will get to know each other first
I foresee awkward conversations in crowded coffee shops
Dates that we won't call dates
I hope you will truly like coffee and not just pretend for me

When we finally touch
Our hands won't fit perfectly like the books say
It will be a slippery mess
My palm will glisten with perspiration
Streams of fear and nervousness but lots of joy
I hope yours will be warm and strong /tethering me
And that will be enough to not let go.
We will hug
You will smell of aftershave mixed with a distinct scent of cologne
And maybe I will smell of old tears /HUMAN.

When we finally kiss
Maybe it will be underneath the glow of the stars or under the scrutiny
of the scorching sun.
But our lips will meet somewhere between what we know and what
escapes us.
Somewhere that echoes you and me.

Sweet laced with nerves and awkwardness
I will taste remnants of mint on your tongue while you will taste toffee
mixed with blackberry juice on mine
Our teeth will knock once or twice and we will burst out with laughter
to ease the nerves.

When we finally make love
I will feel you in all the parts of me that I no longer thought existed.
You will inhale my moans like they are the air you have been craving
for.
Your skin an empty canvas where I will carve my poetry
And we will make a perfect puzzle with the pieces of each other.
And we will hold each other until our ribs vibrate love.

When we die
That is saying one of us
The ocean and skies will weep for you and carry my tears
The lost soul in mine will close her eyes
Remembering how your fire filled kisses had made my scars fade away.
The persistent ache in my soul inhaling the wind that carries the scent
of your memory.
Just maybe then I will be able to let you go.

Wazvionera
Natasha Tinotenda Gwiriri

Ndaikuti teerera wedangwe, zvauri kukura
Uchasangana nezvakawanda, iwe ukati kwete.
Ndichikuudza ini baba vako ukati haiwawo
Ko ivo vakadini ivo vanaye wani mukadzi ,
Iwe kanganwei kuti akuruma nzeve ndewako
Muchengetedze nemwoyo wose kwenguva dzose.

Hezvo nhasi unongomhanyira pamakumbo angu
Misodzi chururu sechana chidiki, wave kuchema.
Mhandara yangu, aiwa chinyarara zvako mwanangu,
Asi chiziva ndambakuudzwa akaonekwa nembonje,
Heyo mbonje iya yave kukutadzisa kurara, uchisvimha.

Ndichagodini semubereki, rega ndipuruzire ronda
Dzamu rasiiwa nomumwe wako rikasikire kupora.
Ndiyo yatinoti kura uzvionere pamhuno sefodya,
Kuti kurarama uku, haiwa haisi nyore mwanangu,
Kunenge mudzanga unoti uku warumwa uku wotsva,
Zvino zvawasangana nazvo, chinyeurirawo vamwe,
Uvanyeurire vasazofamba murima rerudo sezvawakaita.

Experience

Natasha Tinotenda Gwiriri
Translated from Shona by Oscar Gwiriri

All the time I forewarned you
About the tribulations of life,
As a child, you took it for granted
And thought it was an old man's talk,
You based on my past failures
Forgetting he that heeds you wisdom
Is a friend in need and a friend in deed.

Today you lay on my lap once again,
Like a small child, you sob uncontrollably,
Dry those sweet tears dear daughter.
I forewarned you and forearmed you,
It doesn't matter that you made a mistake,
The mistake of love heart breaks anybody.

With parental love, I soothe the heartbreak
Wishing you a speedy recovery of the heart,
Experience is the best teacher of them all,
Now you see, life is not a bed of petals
You bear the suffering of a smoking cigar.
Spread word to other infatuated teenagers,
Forewarn them of matters of the heart and hurt.

WHY SOME MEN LOVE WATER FOR REASONS MORE THAN DRINKING

Nkosiyazi Kan Kanjiri

A man does not need a whole city u
to become a vagabond.
He needs only a heart with holes
to be a permanent wanderer
Because he is a fugitive,
climbing in and out of holes in search of love.

Men who carry perforated hearts
love water for reasons more than drinking.
They love it because they wish they were it,
So they could flow without breaking into pieces
And fill every hole where love resided.

Optimistic Vision
Sheila Banda

Optimism and vision journeyed together
Their companionship inseparable and unquestionable
With labour caked hands and artistic soles
Their destination marked for all to see but for a few to decipher
They trudged along with their rickety cart, wheels creaking but moving

Bags of purpose holding the fort in all four corners,
A pivot to steady the vehicle of change
Drums of hope closely lined the carts' edges
So as to gulp a cup or two, a bottle or two
When their souls were parched
Pots of wisdom centrally positioned
With envelopes of love strewn all over
Calabashes of sunlight planted in any seemingly bare space
For like a passing soothing breeze, wisdom enticingly caressed their
ears and whispered….

….that a titbit of sunlight would they require
If need was there to continue and the way seemed dark
That a ray of sunlight would they require,
When the day was cloudy,
To warm them up just enough.
That a burst of sunlight to be released,
When lonely and downtrodden
For where there's light life buds.

A blanket of perseverance to cover the load

To blind the prying eyes of curiosity
And to protect it from the dust of pessimism
For where pessimism barricades
Optimism removes roadblocks
Where optimisms' flowers nourish and blossom in the rain
Weeds grow in pessimisms garden.

Jealous slanders thrown, for it is so to men of deeds
But a transcendent God gave them a spirit
To annoy their enemies by forgiving
They offered their vulnerability through love
With hurt served for them, they bargained with an envelope of love,
Untainted n' true.

At a snail's pace, they seemed to travel
For vision is not hurried to reach his destination
For whoever hurries is burdened by a goal too huge a task to fulfil!
As they travelled, they marvelled at the bare shrubs
For in due season they would bud & flourish
Under the thorny tree, one day would they find shade
On the dry river bed would their thirst be quenched
At an appointed time when it flows with its' precious golden liquid.

Along the way, tired and hungry
Patches of green grass sprouted
The once deserted road, showing a sign of life
Way ahead, a hazy picture of the future appeared
As in a dream, it seemed flimsy but real
One more step of faith, the veil of uncertainty unmasked
Their Canaan had they reached

Just because when others seemed to lose their heads,
They kept theirs
And came out the tallest of the crowd.
On dreaded giant's shoulders, they rode
Their path being clearer than ever
For boulders seemed as minute stones.

They reached their goal and accomplished their mission
For theirs was a walk of faith to reach a tangible site.

"An optimist is the human personification of spring". Susan J. Bissonette

from a sister to a sister

Sheila Banda

I may not be a perfect sister; but I try
In trying, I may err
Not intentionally as you might think
But in thinking I am doing what's right
It may come out wrong, but l meant it to be right
Can you, in your perfect **time**, right my wrongs
Always hoping that, **that time** will find me there; but
If it doesn't, well,
Just know that in all my imperfections *I LOVE (D) YOU.*

Sharing is caring; that I know
That's why I chose to share this with you
You are a priceless gem
A gem no amount of money can buy
You are a gift
A gift whose value never fades
You are a blessing
A blessing I hope many may realise.

I hope to
>Discover the essence of sisterhood with you
>Uncover the beauty of life with you
>Celebrate every moment in time that God has made for us
>Cherish your dreams..............
We are different but we are one,
Blood never lies and the heart never fails

I am;
joyful of your success
saddened by your sorrow
   gladdened by your achievements
       burdened by your disappointments
       hopeful about your future
amazed by your strength
           always *prayerful* about your life!!

Brothers are brick moulded
Friends are weather moulded
but Sisters are heaven moulded
With their invisible wings always flapping about
Bringing a breath of fresh air
Breathing life to that imperfect part of me.

I hope you will find time to read
For this is from the very bottommost of my heart
This is from me to you,
from a sister to a sister.

Nezvazvo Ndichiri Kungorangarira

Shingirai Manyengavana

Ndarangarira nezvino ,
  Ndichirikungorangarira
  Ndirikungorangarira narinhi,
  Ndicharambandichirangarira.
Marangarirwa nazvino,
  Mucharambamuchingorangarirwa

Makati tizokurangarirai,
  Hezvo nhasi tavakungokurangarirai.
Hatingazombofi takarega kukurangarirai
  Sezvomakati muchazotirangarirawo

Ndarangarira vedzinza rangu inindavarangarira
  Vasharukwa woye toranganapano ,
  Kurangarira uyo mufi
  Nevose vashakabvu vakatisiya
  Ndinokurangarirai mose kwamuri ikoko.

About it, Still I remember.

Shingirai Manyengavana

I remember it even today,
So I will tomorrow and forever.
I will remember.

You asked for remembrance,
And so we remember,
Never hoping to stop,
As you promised to do the same .

I remember my tribe
O men of valor
We have gathered here
To remember our gone beloved
And all those who left us,
We remember you
Wherever you are.

A TALE OF 3 AT 3AM
Thamsanqa Wuna

Taiteyi
Inevitably he awakes,
He won't check the time, He knows,
He half opens his swollen eyes,
As the hole in his heart grows.
He re-lives the horror once more,
Tossing and turning in his dreams,
Inner demons torment him,
And he remembers her screams.
He reaches for the shelf,
He pops another prescription pill,
That's the only way he can cope,
Because depression is very real.

Mai Shupi
His snoring irks her.
Alcohol reeks with every breath,
She detests him tonight,
One day he'll bash her to death.
God; if she could smother him,
Snuff him out and his drooling,
But leaving the kids fatherless?
Oh Lord; who is she fooling?
But one day she will pack up,
This abusive marriage has run its course,
One day she will leave him,
Despite the ignominy of divorce.

Doctor

He's worried, he really is.
He's concerned about his patients,
He's concerned about everyone,
Especially those suffering from depression.
There are those who don't even know,
Those who hurt but never share,
They don't know they're depressed,
And they remain unaware.
Depression is real, it exists,
People suffer from it each day,
At 9am he'll treat Mai Shupi,
And later on it is Taiteyi.

But here's a twist in the tale,
Here's an interesting factor,
They're all up at 3am
But who will treat the doctor?

What is Art?
Thuthukani Ndlovu

Is it the most expensive painting?
The most popular theatre production?
The most captivating poem, song or dance?
Or the most intricate craft,
And can its true value be really measured with money?

I know that my perspective, may not be the same as yours,
But I'm sure that we can all agree that,
Art, is when expression is fused with application,
To produce creative skills that help us emulate our own imaginations.

So what exactly is Art to you?
And why do you call yourself an artist?

There are so many art forms,
So we should not be divided by
Which ones we think are the easiest and the hardest,
For just like Ananda said;
"The artist is not a special kind of person,
Rather each person is a special kind of artist"

Orson Welles said;
"The enemy of Art,
Is the absence of limitations."
So I believe that we should not limit our minds,
Because Art is a communication tool,
That allows us to speak in the most exquisite and common languages,

Even after the end of our lives.

Jars of Ink
Troy Da Costa

The sun rises on the crusted streets
Where wilted flowers lie in rows
And beasts roam on gilded leash
With razor blades on their blooded feet

A Nation grows on those streets
Men like the fruit of trees
I watch them kick and dangle
From one payslip to the next

There were songs to be sung of such a place
But words don't ever come cheap
And all the Inkwells are long dry
So I dip my pen into my wounds because there is no other way to write

A Room with a View

Troy Da Costa

He touches her hair through the curtainless morning sunlight
To make sure she's really there
Her name is Happy
And together they would be forever
A pair of dreamers awakened to each other's arms
There would be a thousand African sunrises
But none like this
Because he is in love for the first time
His heart blossoms in that moment
The taste of her name on his lips
Like a song he could never stop singing.

The Words I Love you

Troy Da Costa

The words, "I Love you"
Are the most gratuitous expression of human emotion
An emotion powerful enough to send stars shooting through the galaxy
And pluck souls from the ether of nonexistence
Yes Love is the brightest light in our heavens
Beyond the reach of the chaos of our waring selves
Our unjust nature
Our desire to cause each other pain
And as the scythe wielder of time catches up with me
To scatter my atoms to the cosmos
I hope it is with these words that he sends me
I Love you

Kwazisano

Tinashe Muchuri

Mhoroi.
Makadiivo?
Takasvunura, makadii?
Tinofara, rakadiiboka?
Rinosvunura, vakadiivamwevavo?
Vanoseka, ndiwomushana wadiikutibvuraudza!
Mukatikunobudachinhu here muminda rwendo rwuno?
Takaona nemichero kupwatsa, tikati zvinemashura izvi.
Zvakasirebwa wani kuti shura rinotangamberi.
Zvichida vane rukweza, mapfunde nemhunga ndivo vachacheka.
Muchidaro here?
Kana ava vane mumera midiki inogona kubatwa nemakuti aKukadzi.
Tongotarisairo denga.
Vachenjeri ndevanototanga kushuzha iyezvino.
Taurai henyu, kumber izvinenge zvorumamutengo.
Izano rakanaka, imiwoye, regai ndiende ndindobvukutirawo zvangu.
Kusakura iyezvino kwavakutopisambesa.
Kungondorinda ndichiona zvichiendanezuva, ungadi usinediridziro?
Hapana.
Zvakanakai regai tiribudire nekupanda kwaro.
Mundovafarisa.
Zvakanaka!

Meeting
Tinashe Muchuri

Greetings to you.
How are you?
We are well and how are you?
We are well and how is your family?
The family is well how is yours?
They are happy except for this troubling drought.
Do you think we will harvest anything this year?
The plenty fruits this season foretold the bad omen.
Bad omen are foretold, our elders didn't the say that?
Maybe those who grow finger millet, sorghum and millet will get a
smile.
Do you think so?
Maybe also those with late crops which may receive the February
showers!
We wait and see what the sky holds for us.
The wise are those who buy and store grain before harvest.
True, after harvest they will be expensive.
A good idea let me go and plough my fields too.
Hoeing the weeds now weakens the plants.
Let me go and watch as the sun depletes them,
What can I do without irrigation?
Nothing!
Anyway, let us set out in heat.
Greet them for us.
It is well.

Mukutaura kwake anoti

Tinashe Muchuri

Akangoti mudzimai waMagodo ishamwariyake
Haana kana chaanoziva uyo
Mbudzi mbiri dzangoinda pachena
Haaana chaakaita Madhombiro

Kup ikwawakanzwa murume anoita shamwari yemukadzi wemunhu?
Handiti ndiwo mavambo ekufuka jira risirako
Muridzi otiwasvibisa jira rangu, iwe wotihwava handizvo!
Unoripa, kuwana ovaka ushamwari, zvakatanganepi?

Iye unotimudzimai waMagodo akangwarira pane zvebudiriro
Munhu asigaririmaoko ake
Anoshandira mhuri murume achitevera kwaradirwa
Iko kwaanodzoka kana haridzasukwa.

Iye wakoMadhombiro akati ndini ndavababazve!
Hino wapaona pane mukore wachozve!
Zvekusiyadzasukwa zvineinaye?
Ko, kana kurikutenderana kwavo?

Dare rakonewa haro kutonga.
Ushamwari imhosva sekuti vabatwa varimumagudza?
Kungotaura kutimudzimai waMagodo ishamwari yatovemhosva!
Madzishe anoda kudya zvavanhu pachena.

Iye ndiye akada kudyirwafuma pachena.
Zvizivire mumoyo mune ushamwari hwenyu.

95

Kududza paruzhinji kupupura wakautora mudzimai wemuridzi.
Usafa wakarasha muromo kudero pajikerere.

Kubva iye haana mufaro nazvo.
Kutotuma vanhu kusvika kwavanga vasativasvikazve!
Unozokona here iwe watotorerwafuma yako pasina?
Handiti ndipo panozonzi kusikufa ndekupi?

Muudze agarire kure nemunhu wavanhu.
Nhasi dzaindambudzi nhatu neyedare yagochwa.
Mangwana ratovadanga kuripa yerooro yakainda kwabambo.
Mudzimai wemuridzi haabatwi hama.

Kubva ndichamuudza tione kana akazvisiya
Asi munhu anofarira vanoshanda nesimba kuti vasimudzirane.
Kwete simbe vanamutevera kwaradirwa.
Hameno kana akazvigashira!

Akaita ndambirira hameno hake.
Dzinongoinda dzichikuma nepaasina kunanzva.
Imwe igogochwa dare rigozipirwa nenharodzake.
Ini wangu muromo mwiro.

He said

Tinashe Muchuri

He said Magodo's wife is his friend
He knows more than their friendship
But was made to pay two goats as fine
He did nothing wrong, Madhombiro

Where have ever heard a man who befriends someone' wife?
Isn't that begging of infidelity?
The husband says you have eaten my fruit, and you deny!
You will be punished, they will ask, how did the friendship started?

He is saying Magodo's wife is an entrepreneur and a development agent
She doesn't sit on her laurels
She wins for the family while her husband hunts for seven day brew
Where he returns all the calabashes are empty and clean

So your Madhombiro decided to cover for him!
You see where the problem is!
What has his beer drinking to do with him?
What if it is their covenant?

The court was biased.
How can it punish friendship, as if they were caught between the blankets?
If just saying Magodo's wife is my friend a crime!
Our chiefs are corrupt; they want to plunder their servant's wealth.

He is the fool who traded his wealth for nothing.

Keep your friendship a secret.
Confessing it in public is as good as saying you are in love with someone's wife.
Don't ever say such words in public.

But he is not happy about it.
It is setting up people into the path they were not intending to traverse.
Do you think you will restrain yourself when you are punished for a crime you did not commit?
Isn't it that you will be forced to take the bull by the horns?

Just tell him to stay away from someone's wife.
Today three goats have gone, two for the husband and the third we roasted at the court.
If he keeps on, he will be asked to restitute half the lobola that Magodo paid for.
Don't ever befriend someone's wife.

Will warn him and see if he agrees
But he is a person who appreciates and support hard work.
Not the lazy seven day brew hunters.
Will try, only if he sees sense in it!

If he keeps on, beware.
Cattle will go though he is not sleeping with her.
And another one will be roasted by the court for nothing.
Let me be silent and watch.

People First
Tinashe Muchuri

to die of Cholera and Typhoid
People first
to die of hunger and starvation
people first
to suffer the wrath of sanctions
people first
to be detained and tortured
people first
to lose their shelter because its dirty
people first
to be killed by potholed roads
people first
to be cut off of electricity and water
people first
to die experience the impact of HIV/AIDS
people first
to pay the pain of corruption
people first
to endure mismanagement of national resources
people first
to feel the aching after political violence
people first
to lose their belongings through politically motivated violence
why should they not be the first
to enjoy independence and peace of the world?

Take out the trash.

Nyashadzashe Chikumbu

Midnight summer nightmares
I woke up sneezing
Coughing dust, chocking on asbestos
The night's sky had cracked perfervid red.
Midnight crises
I woke up to a nightmare
Not blood bursting as an incubus bedding your wife.
But lung-clotting as tuberculosis
The asbestos, corrugated iron roofing bars
Had liquefied raining on my bed.
My lungs refused to breath
O, I wished I had gills or I would have
Swan in the ocean of rebel.
The bulldozer stopped-painting, raised another fist and stroke again,
The shack that once was my crown gave in...
It rained bricks, it rained blood
It was a midsummer nightmare.

Broken things

Nyashadzashe Chikumbu

Where do broken things go?
Rotting biopsy bags are not for land-fills.
Flies and maggots they spread like a cancer eating the flesh.
Dogs, vipers dimwitted brides
Outside they belong where the cold pills the enamel off your teeth,
spooking your bones to a gnashing frenzy.
Where do broken things go?
Witches do you burn them
Or cast them in the evil forests to dance with the age old twins and lost
albinos'?
I'll ask again, where does a broken people with lose morals hanging like
a toddler's underwater go?
The world burns does no one care?

Police brutality

Artwork © by Tendai R Mwanaka

Dear Emerson Mnangagwa:
Free and Fair Elections!
Tendai Rinos Mwanaka

"What is your name, Skull?"

There are a couple of years at school I want to talk to you about. There is the year we got a really difficult insufferable Head boy at school. He was too strict. Even if you were friends with him, if he found you on the wrong end of the school rules, he will book you for punishment. And I had my full share of these bookings and detentions. Yes, I admit I was a difficult student. But what I also realized, even for those who were never punished by this head boy, they still didn't like him. Deep down all this insufferable strictness, he was driven by a streak of cruelty. He wallowed in cruelty. The students finally realized this about him. Even on issues where the whole student body was fighting against the administrators, he always found his side with the administrators, yet his other job was to represent the students to the powers that be. So the students ended up resenting him. The students liked his deputy who was a far better person, wished the deputy was the one at the top. This deputy treated us as adults, respectfully. But the deputy never got the chance to lead us. With the end of this head boy's term of office we selected another head boy. What the old head boy had made us feel was that office was against the students; we distrusted it, so that this new head boy took off with a student body that already despised the office he was taking over. We didn't give him time to adjust, and show us what he was all about. We distrusted him straight off. We shut him out, we resented him. And he responded exactly like the previous head boy. He punished us. He blocked us. He harassed us and we wished his deputy would get a chance to lead us. But the deputy can only become the head boy only if the head boy leaves his office during his term of office. At school that was highly unlikely, so we had to figure out a way to deal with that, and moved on with our lives.

Emerson, you are the second head boy at this school we are enrolled in for all our lives. This school has a name; Zimbabwe. Emerson you have inherited an office that we despise, that we don't like because that office was made a monster by Robert Mugabe. It is so offensive to us. Robert used that office to punish us, to kill us, to maim us, to destroy out economy and country, to make us feel like we were nobodies in our school. It's only him we had to listen to and obey. We learned to hate Robert and the office of the president. Don't be fooled into thinking we only hated Robert. We hated the whole system, the whole government. We never wished for you to take over like we wished those deputy head boys to take over at school so many moons ago. You were Robert. You are Robert. Here is a tale I want to share with you, Emerson

Some time ago, not so long ago there was this man who felt he had shadows he didn't understand. He told himself there were shadows that spoke to him when he was asleep but never really grasped what they wanted him to do. And then they started to speak to him even when he was awake, when he was listening, when he wasn't listening. He heard those shadows speaking deep inside himself. The voices of which were an amalgam of light and shadows flickering, sizzling him with restlessness he didn't understand or know how to deal with. They told him he had to go to a Well by the end of the village, a disused, dumped Well, where naught kids circled, around the close of the day, singing, calling the old prophet to come and awash them with gold. There is a story, a legend that the Well had dried in another lifetime with the

104

death of an old prophet man of this village when he fell in this Well and died in this well. It was said the prophet man had tried to retrieve a blood tree (Mubvamaropa tree) box that was full of gold. So that, even when the villagers managed to retrieve the dead body of this prophet, it was thought the Well was cursed, yet some thought a ceremony dance around this Well helped to soften the restless and hunger inside souls, a hunger of wealth. These kids were propagating this folklore, though playfully, but in this old man the voice kept whispering to him to go to the Well. It told him that deep inside the Well there was definitely a Mubvamaropa tree box full of treasures. The voice told him to go to the Well and excavate this treasure trove.

This man, deep in his dreams left for the Well. He knew he had to listen to this voice and free himself from its restlessness. He had to go there to find wealth for himself and his people. In this night the moon was a bruise on the skies, it emitted reddish wounds of flowers of light, the whole night was in bubbles of voices beckoning, wishing him to keep going, to keep moving, and he could only obey these voices. He couldn't make himself to stop. He got to this Well in the early hours of morning. It was surreal, he searched around for the rope the people of that far off time had used to excavate the old prophet man with and he found it was still there, waiting for him like one left over log to use to light up a fire in a world with no trees. He took a small stone and threw it into the Well to measure how deep the Well was; by noting the time it took for the stone to hit the box of treasure. The thumb hit of this mubvamaropa tree told him the rope was long enough to reach the bottoms. He immersed the rope with a hook attacked to its end into the Well. He felt it hit something and he felt it hook it. He starts drawing it out. He felt the weight. He knew he had finally rounded up on his voices. The expectations he had for the treasures! He kept drawing it until something hang on top of the Well's mouth. It had the

105

shape. Not of a box! He reached his hand to touch it, to see it. He was asleep so he couldn't really see it with his shut eyes, but he used his fingers to feel it, to see it. His hands closed on this object. He touches two holes on its top; and a opening below them belies a mouth. He knew it was the skull he was holding. He asks this skull,

WHAT'S YOUR NAME, SKULL? But the skull didn't answer him. He was angry and like Moses throwing the tablets on the ground in the bible, he threw it on the ground. He cried to the space above him

WHERE IS MY BOX OF WEALTH, WHY DID YOU SEND ME THIS SKULL?

Nothing answers him. He takes the skull in his hands, he looks at it again with his fingers, and he felt a song in his heart telling him it was the skull of his mentor. The skull looked familiar, like his head on his body. He touches his head, he felt he was touching his mentor's head. So he looked at the skull again and tears begun flowing down his face. The front porch of his brain knew he was himself in this skull. He was the skull. He asks the skull again, softly.

What is your name, Skull?

He only heard his own voice askance.

He took the skull and put it on his head, and it fitted him well. He knew he was the skull.

This is how we know you are the skull. It is your story's life, Emerson. Don't ask us how we came to know of this, we only know! This is how we know you are Robert. This is how we know we are dealing with Robert's skull. No, Emerson we are not going to give you time. No, I have no reason to think you will be different from your skull. Don't forget we know you were with Robert at the Well trying to excavate the box full of wealth in Marange, and that you helped him

106

make us hate the office of the president, the government. Don't be surprised when everything you do or touch is going to create noise, anger, bitterness and displeasure with the people. What are the sounds for but to hear what isn't there. It's your voice you will be hearing.

Dear president, our apologies, we will chop you off the living skull on your head.

You are Robert Mugabe. It's you who hurt us for 37 years. It's you who destroyed the country for 37 years. The country is empty. I think if I were to go home now and knock on the Zimbabwean blue skies, I would hear the hallow sound of my own empty hands penning this missive in all that Zimbabwean blue. It's you who stole the elections for 37 years; it's you who burned down our homes, maimed people who were against you. If you think I am fibbing go to Kwekwe today and ask the people there what they think of you. Ask the Kwekwe people who burned down Blessing Chebundo's home, who killed a number of activists in Kwekwe. Emerson, it's you who killed thousands of the Matabele people. Despite the fact that you are always saying it's not you who led the genocide, ask the Matabele people who killed their families. They know it's you. The whole country knows it's you. Yes, we know they were a lot of people involved in that madness (Sidney Sekeremayi, Perence Shiri, Solomon Mujuru and the army, Edson Shirihuru, Kevin Woods, Menard Muzariri, the CIO people, and you Emerson, Robert Mugabe, his deputies and cabinet, even Chiwengwa... all these a closeted plausibility of chihauhaus, come back Joshua Nkomo!). Oh, Chiwenga can as well say what you saying too, to excuse himself since he was at the 1 Infantry Brigade in Bulawayo not the monster 5 Infantry brigade based in Kwekwe that Perence Shiri lead as they grounded down the Matebele people. Chiwengwa provided support to Shiri's 5 Brigade. You two can say you were not there when you were there, but we all know it's a lie. Even a wind takes with it evidence of where it has been. Violence is a product of systemlessness as much as a pillar of lootercracy, Emerson. Who did the target killing of the politicians and leaders of the Gukurahundi? It's the CIO. Who tried to kill Nkomo as he skirted out of the country in woman dressing, running from your thugs the CIO who were on his tail. You were the minister of security, Emerson. Tell us why Mugabe fired you, if you were not involved. Don't think we are such fools we will accept you didn't know what your subordinates like Kevin Woods were doing in the ministry you led. Don't think we are dump goats we don't know the army couldn't have done that work without the intelligence knowledge it got from the CIO. It is the CIO that helped the army extirpates the Matabele. You were the head of the organisation, you crushed them in your hands, you are covered in blood that dripped from the people to become empty shells, like testimony. So don't tell us lies, no amount of lies will ever make us think of you differently as your skull, Robert. A caterpillar out of botulism does not become a butterfly. So stop trying to persuade us you are clean, prove it. Come out clean. Tell us what really happened in Matabeleland. This experiment is to see who has been killing us, Emerson. The experiment is about a lot I don't know, the experiment is about silent things talking in the dark of now. You are Robert and the Zimbabweans have no engagement rings for you man; they can't commit themselves to a thug boss!

Emerson, it's you who killed your rivalries and Robert's rivalries in the ZANUPF power soaps we have come to expect over the years. It is you who has pushed out those who blocked your ambitions to one day succeed Robert and come to terms with your voices inside you. It's you who we blame for the killing of Solomon Mujuru, Learnmore Jongwe, the generals, the political commissars (Movern Mahachi, Elliot

Manyika, Border Gezi), and everyone who was against your ambitions and your skull, Robert. It's you we blame for everything that Zimbabwe is; oh we might as well blame you for global warming! Let my pen reveal what you can't reveal to us and if I am free to speak loosely, the predator could easily be revealed. It's you who forced Robert to take farms from the whites, you who gutted the white people. Don't think you can fool us now when you say you have changed, that you now want the white people back. An eagle no matter how much it cleans itself is always black. Do you know each pattern is different, like a snowflake but none is as cold as you are? It's you who pushed Robert to send our soldiers to the DRC to fight a war that has never benefited the generality of Zimbabweans, but rather depleted every foreign currency reserve the country had and pushed us into inflation. It's you who looted the DRC of its diamonds and made billions out of that Lootercracy. Ask the United Nations, they know your money was from blood diamonds you looted in the DRC and at that Well in Marange. It's you Emerson who stole elections that the opposition had won in 2008. Wasn't that you we heard who told your skull that he wasn't going anywhere, and took the whole country to ransom as you played with the work of our pens until Chiwenga's gun ruled us again? Emerson, it's you who helped create the securocratic leadership style that now subject us to poverty, it's you who re-created the monster Joint Operations Command that has run the country, *de facto* basis since year 2000.

It's you Emerson who took the country through a coup just a few weeks ago, and hauled your skull to the ground. You opened your big mouth which can only be described as that of a comic book character, gulped everything down at once. Didn't we hear you from foreign lands asking the skull what his name was? Didn't we hear your voice in the voice of your chummy Chiwenga asking Robert who his name was whilst his distance from our streets disagrees with us, by imprisoning Robert in his beautiful blue roof casket? With frightening speed, actions took hold of Robert in a matter of a few days. Didn't you repeatedly lie to us that it wasn't a coup, didn't you say it had no name. You called it operation restore order, you called it a coup which was not a coup, you called it capturing thieves surrounding the president, so why did you capture the skull into your hands and took it to be yours, why did you fit the skull on your head at the end of the coup. Yes, there was so much love lost between Robert and us. We had buried our love of Robert so many years ago like that village had buried the body of their prophet who had died in that Well. We supported you, we danced around the Well with you Emerson, and we were little children looking for something we didn't know, whittling away at the silhouette that had kept us captive so that the night of his resignation we all might sail into drinks and talk and the shared adulations of this small army of joy, the vibrations, the vibe, buzz, bizz bizz, the fear, and in the morning the sweepers would follow the parade march. But you hijacked that dream for us too. Even though we danced with you we knew the Well was not clean. We knew you were not clean. We supported you because we felt it was better to deal out one monster at a time. Now Robert is gone, don't think we are fools to think his Mugabeism is buried with his body, no. You have his skull on your head, Emerson. We still see the shadows. We know ZANUPF is a group of look alikes/ dress alikes/ think alikes/ looter alikes, near insanity Bono rock music look alikes who concocted to distance themselves from their boss when the people called it quits, and your ZANUPF supporters even know you are interchangeable, and that when these look alikes are kicked, other Robert Mugabe look alikes will take over like allusions of the Mussolinis eating Ethiopian checken

110

(chicken) bones in the form of the Mengestus. You are just a new leader of an old sect. We even know you are more dangerous than Robert; that Mugabe's imaginations have hybridized into monster crops in you! Yet it's better to deal with the head of the snake than its tails that we have been doing all along. Now, you are out on the open.

We are going to fight you until you are gone too. We are on you, until we eat your footsteps in our sleep. I cast out a proud call to you Emerson; we will swallow stones, grasses, poison, bitterness, molasses, stuff our mouths with emptiness, depth and height for the next few months until the elections. Emerson, we will consume birds, beasts, locusts, monsters, fish, glue, sadza, wind clay salt, ripples…, until we become this for you, stone and only stone, until we push you out too. We know it is good to be alive, even on a leash, to test our reflexes. You are from ZANUPF. So as far as we concerned we gave you 37 years and you rundown the country. 37! 37! 37! We are not going to give you another 37 years to ruin us further. We have waited too long for uhuru, and the georgics of waiting beyond now are time as a torn cloth. We know you have nothing to offer us. We know you can only resort to buying our votes in the next 8 months or so until the elections. We see you have started the "buying us" programme. You think it impresses us that you have refused to use Robert's chariot of fire, the limousine, gold plated with the black gold of the blood he bleed from us over the years as he paraded and cocked all over our roads. Of course your emergence demand a makeover that would seem to impart change, simplicity and maturity, perhaps a whiff of Africa's present darling, a magufulication! If you think it impresses us you cut back your congress expenditure from 8 mil to 2 mil. If you think we have bought into those promises you made that you are now born again and should be absolved for killings you did under Robert, and

111

that you now want the white people back, now that you have the crown, making it seem as if it was Mugabe only who was wrong all along. If you wanted this done you should have done it yesterday. Everyone knows Mugabe was against farm invasions, tried to fight you and the goons to leave the farms. If you think we can easily buy into this fluffy thing that you now want to compensate the whites for taking their farms forcefully, with what money, Emerson. I will come to that later (letter). If you want it done right now put pride aside man, and tell us the truth and pray to space. Achieve a better form of purity, Emerson! If you think we have bought into your lies that you now want to resuscitate the economy you destroyed, that you have started by cutting down the number of ministries in your government, and if I may ask you, why is there some process toward militarizing the government. This unassembled cabinet that is waiting for its own loot in this mineral rich country! I might come back to that, no promises. Emerson, just know that all that you have done or purporting you will do doesn't impress us. First thing first, Emerson!

We have an election next year. Make that right, first of all. Give us a free and fair election. Win or lose it fairly, then if you win fairly we will start trusting your good intentions. Rest awhile; we are not even there yet, not even with a fair election. There are sins you have to apologize and pay for, for humankind's swelling expenses. I will come to that later. Let's stay on the elections now. I said we know all these promises were to buy us into believing you now care for us as we toward the elections. Whereas your skull gave us food and agric implements, sometimes used panties to cloth up our open business, you thought you could better your skull by offering us what we have clamored for all along to fill up our flesh, thus to flesh up your skull too. I said we know you are not the deputy head boy of this school. You are Robert, the head boy!

On free and fair elections here are the areas I want you to right. Fire Rita Makarau and her gang at ZEC. We know she is the dust that clung around the skull you have in your hands. She is Robert's lapdog, she stole the 2013 election for Robert, awarding him and his party ZANUPF the two thirds majority they now have. Just think of it. How could your old decaying skull get a two thirds majority in a village that so hated the shadows of your skulls. No, she has to go. The second issue is ZEC should be totally independent, chosen by civil society institutions like the Judiciary Service Commission, or be chosen by the Parly, with equal representation of parties that constitute our Parly. Not by the executive, not by the immediate players, not by oncoming players. The Registrar General is another public office that needs to be removed from your tentacles. Let's have the Parly overseeing that one too, or the judiciary.

The next reform area is on the military and security establishment. Zimbabwe is now a blank terrain, surrounded by two armies, one wields a gun and another, a pen. We want the army off our political processes. Tell Chiwenga and his power grabbing goons to go back to the barracks. Tell those monsters to focus their energies on military issues, not political processes. We need a law that makes it clear that its treason for the army to enter our streets to temper with political process, payable by jail sentence. If they have nothing to do at the barracks, they should help in the construction of schools, clinics, roads etc. If they are tired of mooching off our taxes, if they are tired of training without a fight to engage in, export them to the world over, the world is full of strife. It would earn us foreign currency. Employ them to farm the millions of hectors that remain uncultivated every year and grow our agricultural industry and other industries. Apparently those goats are employable and there is a lot that needs to be done to build back Zimbabwe. They should leave politics to politicians, law to lawmakers and judiciary, theirs is military. We don't have a war in Zimbabwe. Nobody is killing the other in Zimbabwe. Zimbabwe has next to nothing possibility of degenerating into a war situation like Somalia which your chummy used as the cry call to enter the streets. We are civilized. We don't kill each other in Zimbabwe. This is not bloody Central or West Africa! Emerson, the military needs to be reformed, and those who have nothing to do should be retired. The heads of the military have to be retired too. We need new thinking, fresh perspectives in this organisation. We have over 30 000 active soldiers- that's too much for a country as small a Zimbabwe, a country that has no possibility of generating a war. What do we need all those soldiers for? There is nobody in the SADC region who wants to attack us, we don't even have any territorial dispute with any country in the SADC. And on top of that we have over 22 000 reserve soldiers in the form of war veterans, and these have been used to destabilize us, destroy opposition parties and make Zimbabwe ungovernable by messing with our political processes. Retire all these veterans, too. They have no use. Those who want to be politicians, let them do that on a personal level, not using our taxes to rape us further. We need a small highly technological and advanced force that focuses on their mandates in the constitution. It's no longer a game of numbers nowadays. Look at American wars for the last few years. They are winning fights without deploying a lot of soldiers on the ground. Cull this lot. We need about 15 000 soldiers for the size of Zimbabwe. Still on security reforms, the police and civil security establishment needs reforms. Their mandates are to protect the civilians and uphold the law. They should move from the police state that they are now and have made Zimbabwe to be, into a people state police. The CIO should focus on country security not politicians security, or party games that they are involved in.

The next reform area I want see done before the elections is on the media. Open up the airwaves. Licence more players in this important field. Make this "fourth organ" of state strong and independent. We need new independent broadcasters. For us to still have 1 TV station, 37 years down the line is an insult to us. For us to still have only 6 national radio stations that are all controlled by the government, one way or another is an insult. For us to have very few local community radio stations is simply bad. Open up the airwaves and leave the journalists and media people to do their jobs in a free and fair environment, not to report according to party lines. ZANUPF is not Zimbabwe. I know that because I didn't see the memo that changed Zimbabwe to be ZANUPF republic. The media's job is to serve the people not politicians. Allow free and fair reporting on the national broadcaster, give competing parties into the next year's elections fair share of airwaves time. Leave the internet alone. Leave people to express what they think in these internet social platforms. Let the information be shared in a free and fair way. It's laughable you have a ministry that focuses on that. I wonder what flimsy ministry you are going to create next, the ministry for love!

The other reform area is on the commission that deals with constituency demarcation. The job should be given to an independent organisation, independent from your executive power mongering hands. The constituency delimitation and demarcation should be overseen by Parly or judiciary appointed organization. We know how you have used this exercise to give yourself and your party unfair advantage over opposition parties. This is how you got two thirds majority in the Parly now. How did I come to this when I am not a statistician? When I realized the impossibility of counting to infinity the millions in Zimbabwe, I have decided to vomit these numbers. It's a big flat joke to think that a city like Chitungwiza that crawls with people from every hole, over 1.5 million people, will have 5 constituencies, yet a district like Gokwe will have the equal number of constituencies. And this capital should be damned- Harare, which has plus 2 million people has not more than 20 constituencies yet provinces with fewer people than Harare have more constituencies. Don't lie to us that three major urban centers (Harare, Chitungwiza and Bulawayo) with more than 4 million people combined together would not even have a fifth of the constituencies of Zimbabwe. 4 million people is almost a third of Zimbabwe's population. Protest all you want, but there is a grain of truth in these vomits. Let the statistician illuminate this beyond mathematical doubt, if you want. We know you and your party have used this organisation to give more constituencies to rural areas that have more ZANUPF supporters than those that are predominantly opposition. Get your power mongering hands off this cake, Emerson.

The next port of call is the judiciary. I find a judiciary that legitimatizes a coup suspect. A coup is a coup, that's the only name it is known by; otherwise we might as well call it a soup. We all stumbled as we were struck in the shock of it! But a simple truth is soldiers in a constitutional democracy can only come into the streets in times of war or civil emergences, not to right a party. Chiwenga was clear why he decided to enter our streets from the beginning of it. He wanted to clean up the mess in the ZANUPF party, period. What happened later with major general SB Moyo is known as sanitizing a wrong. I have said it before ZANUPF is not a country. Why didn't he enter the streets to right the MDC when it had power problems? We have an election to sort the country, not the army. And the sick thing is if a judiciary is

116

blind to how the law works, how are we going to have faith in such an institution like that. Chiwenga is not the commander-in-chief of Zimbabwe Defense Forces. Mugabe was the boss. So for Chiwenga to come into our streets it had to be signed off by the president. It was Mugabe who had the right to allow the soldiers to invade the streets and break down government as they did. It doesn't matter if it was for the right causes or wrong causes. It's a wrong precedent the army and courts have set. What if the same army decides, in the future, to invade the streets again without your consent and hold the country by the gun? It's dangerous to have an army that doesn't operate under the country's constitution. There is nothing legal about that coup. So we need an overhaul of our judiciary. We want them to be independent of the executive levers and authority, to be able to safeguard our constitution against the monster that invaded our streets. The military that is bend on instituting what they want on the electorate and a conniving ruling party and cowering judiciary. Make no mistake, Emerson; a day will reckon when someone in your party will use the same army to hold you at gunpoint like they did to Robert and call it a coup that is not a coup, and with a stupid judiciary like the one that has just sanitized the coup this army will remove you from power too.

The other reform area is to do with the electoral law. Let's have an independent justice body that deals with the election contestation issues. Don't forget every time there was a dispute this judiciary has just sat on the cases that the opposition had brought to the courts. None have been dealt with; some never saw a court date. It took the judiciary 5 years to the next election to not decide the 2002, and 2005 election disputes, and then the cases became null and void as another election became due. We need an election body made up of representatives of several facets of the government, country, parties, experts, civil society,

NGOs, local authorities, religious groupings…, and these would decide on elections matters and do so before a president-elect is inaugurated. There is no free and fair election in subjecting the electorate to a president who has won a disputed election.

The last issue I want to touch on is of allowing observers and monitors to observe and monitor our elections. Allow all those who want to come to observe to come. Allow and protect party monitors to monitor elections without fear for their lives. We want to see an election where the opposition can be able to deploy monitors in areas like Muzarabani and Uzumba Maramba Pfungwe without fear for their lives. Without which, don't lie to us and your cohorts of ZANUPF supporters like SADC and AU that the election has been free and fair

These are areas I want to see tackled before elections next year. As you can see, Emerson, it's a lot of work that needs your focus, rather than trite issues like you have refused to use the limousine crap. We know ZANUPF party is a master at deflecting people's views to buy into an illusion that things are now fine to win over their vote. Those are only trapdoors that don't get us home. Mugabe's regime was our knowledge pond: we are graduates revolting.

Code to the core, Mnangagwa you do so move, always you do so move man, to maim us, and now you do so move, you move to soothe us. We know this gimmick; we know this thing about limousine, of catching the said to be thieves is just useless noise. You are hiding from the election reform issues, cradling to your old ways, hiding, stealing, thuggery... If you are really serious about growing Zimbabwe again, do the reforms first and give us a free and fair election for the first time. If you win as I have noted that before we will support you to the hilt as you rebuilt the country you destroyed. It's a museum of things for us to forget too, always afraid we might forget the distance we have travelled, the trouble of stopping now. Oh we can't afford to stop now. There are no stops in these roads of gravel. The angry gestures over our former authorities and current authorities in the letter are only means in the roads we are travelling in. These roads of gravel we are travelling in will lead to freedom of the constructions our dreams. We are in phases of tilling and harvesting, November's rain fire lures us to our freedoms.

We will accept you on one condition! First of all declare what you have, and how you got it. Tell us how much you looted from that Well in Marange. Everyone in your new government should do that too. If you can at least prove to us what happened to the 15 billion you found in that Mubvamaropa box in the Well in Marange, then we will believe all this noise. I said first of all pay back what you stole, show us what you benefited from through corruption, push your cabal in the ZANUPF to declare what they benefited from through corruption, and then the whole country will do likewise. Otherwise this is just a sad excuse you are using to blindfold us to steal an election with, and when you have won then you will revert back to business as usual in something that is continuous, alooter continue. Oh don't confuse democracy and alootercracy, even if they both end in –acy…no, not that! I stop it, I am subjected!

Another gimmick you have narrowed on is the land issue. You know it is an emotional issue. You have promised the white people you are going to pay them for stealing their lands. Who is going to pay for that? I never got a piece of land from that exercise, never stole land from the white people, never benefited from it, in fact the bulk of the country didn't benefit from that, why must our taxes be used to pay for what we never benefited from. Rather the exercise has made the whole country poor. Those who looted the farms must pay the white people for the loot. We are waiting for the land reform audit. Those who have more than 1 farm, must return these to the white people they displaced to loot. They are practically hundreds, if not thousands of these farms that can be returned to their rightful owners before you start making us pay for your looting. How can we Zimbabweans be made to compensate white people to allow people like Robert Mugabe, Edna Madzongwe, Shuvai Mahofa to keep more than 5 farms each, farms they are not even using. Don't forget when you arm twisted your skull to enter the farms and allow your goons to displace the white people you lied to us that you will each only get a farm, not 5, not 14 for one person. If you want to earn our respect, stop subjecting us under taxes we didn't benefit from. It's us people who have suffered from these stupid policies like the land invasion. You meted poverty on us. And we have become who we are and learned how to cry and produce material evidence of our sadness. Don't think we will be patient as you continue subjecting us to this callousness. We are wild now, we are not afraid of your tanks. Look, we are saying, "we are sad", we are hurt enough, and we won't accept more pain. You and your band of crooks benefited from the land reform, so please payback the whites from the rent you have accrued from using those farms for nearly 20 years. There is no excuse why you can't payback the white people what you stole from them. We see this for what it is. It's another election gimmick.

In the meanwhile open up industry, clean up the mess you created with the indigenization programme. Chunk that law into the Robert Mugabe dustbin. Create attractive investment opportunities and environments in the country to allow industry to grow. Create free tax zones in the country. Use the Silicon Valley/ Shanghai method that has made China and the USA super rich, allow investors to invest in tax free heavens, especially companies that employ more people, thus this will cut back on unemployment rates and boast government tax base. Focus on creating solid banking structures in Zimbabwe, stabilize the currency, and control the financial sector. Clean up the mess at the mining sector; make it secure for investments and also secure our taxes from the mining sector. We can't afford to lose another 15 billion dollars. Make tourism and services industries grow. This is an easy cash cow as they are fewer investments involved to make money in this sector, than in industry, mining and agriculture. Clean up our image in the international community. This will encourage more tourists to visit. We have enough tourist attractions sites to make Zimbabwe a world class tourist destination centre.

As you can see there is a lot we want you to do before we warm up to you, and you don't have time or our patience. Of course we will tolerate you for next few months problematically; don't forget a hungry educated pen is both a gun and pen. First of all, and I repeat it, give us free and fair elections!

I think I am a no one or nation and this outrage is justified, there is no purpose of nation if it doesn't allow a frame where happiness zigzags with beauty.

This letter has two distinct cries. One is called Chiduce, an omen of good, and the other is Huitreu, which is extremely unfavourable! Hope you have heard both cries.

Thank you, Ndinotenda, Ngiyabonga

Conversations With John Eppel

Describe yourself in five words?

A left-handed European African.

What is your most treasured possession?

I can't say my children because they aren't possessions so I'll settle for my house in Bulawayo.

Do you have any strange hobbies?

Yes: listening to historical recordings of opera.

What is your greatest fear?

My children and grandchildren getting hurt.

What were you like at school?

Uninterested.

What are you doing next?

Working intermittently on another novel.

Your ex-wife was involved in poetry earlier. How much did you inspire each other back then?

I don't know if 'inspire' is the right word but we certainly supported each other in our creative efforts. Shari was the first Zimbabwean poet to publish a piece on the Fifth Brigade atrocities, a poem called 'Bhalagwe', which was published in the first of 'amaBooks' 'Short Writings' series. That was extremely brave of her.

Can you tell us about your initial encounters with poetry, and initial impressions with writing? What traditions and cultures, writers and artists you have studied and how have these shaped your writing. Tell us about the writing scene in your country.

To start at the end, the writing scene in Zimbabwe is vibrant, especially among the younger generation who are less inclined to censor themselves, more inclined to ridicule those in power who abuse it.

My initial encounters with poetry, as I have said before, were at my segregated primary school where we were mislead by nostalgic expatriates from all corners of Great Britain. However, I loved the poetry they introduced to us, mainly from the Georgian era - poets like Alfred Noyes, John Masefield, and Walter de la Mare. I loved them for their lyricism, and that influence is with me today. Poetry shares content with philosophy, history, religion, psychology, politics.., it is nothing special; but poetry's form is its own.

I got to African literature too late - in my twenties - for it to have much of an influence on my writing. But I was steeped in English literature. The first place I wanted to visit when I finally got to England was Kensington gardens - the world of Peter Pan!

Give us an overview of your published work. What are the issues at the centre of your writing and why

I've always considered myself more of a poet than a prose writer even though I've published more prose than poetry. I first started to get published in the late 60s, along with contemporaries like Charles Mungoshi, Musaemura Zimunya, and the late Julius Chingono. Well, I'm still getting published, still in a fairly unobtrusive way, 50 years later. If I include collaborations, I have had, in that time about 18 books of poetry and prose published.

Most of my prose is satirical, hence its limited appeal; most of my poems are lyrical, with a slightly less limited appeal.

What is your writing process?

Poetry comes to me; I go to prose.

Of the older generation of writers you have collaborated with other writers across cultures in Zimbabwe more than many of your contemporaries, why. What do you enjoy about these collaborative endeavors and how do you go about it.

Poets are kindred spirits. We can sit for hours together without having to say a word, though words are our game. But of course, it's more than that. I'm proud to be published alongside black writers whose work I admire; and I'm grateful too, that after a long dry season I am beginning to be accepted as a Zimbabwean writer.

Tell us about your poems in Zimbolicious Poetry Anthology Volume 1

I think they are typical of my style, and indicate that my subject matter is variable.

If you were a poem, what form will you be in?

The sonnet of course. Ask PAN.

An Interview With Jabulani Mzinyathi

05 JANUARY 2018

When did you begin your career as a literary artist? Can you tell us about your education, both in and outside the classroom?

My first poem was published by Moto Magazine in 1992. That marked the start of my career as a known literary artist. Thanks to the late Onesimo Makani Kabweza who was the editor then. My career as a literary artist had however started from the time I was in Form One at Ascot Secondary School Gweru. I had my school boy love and protest poems tucked away in my book case. I did not know what to do with them. I just wrote on and on. Later in life I became a member of BWAZ Midlands Branch. There I came into contact with Stephen Alumenda, Dillion Banda, Hleko Vuma and many others. I cannot recall at what stage the enigmatic Mbizo Chirasha came onto the scene. Of course Emmanuel Sigauke was there too at some stage. Those were people I came across in the formative years of my literary career!

Education began on the streets of Ascot High Density suburb. There we would meet brothers and sisters who were already at school. It was a joy as they read aloud to us. Mambo Press used to churn out a lot of comics. If I recall well, these revolved around a character called Musa. They were sold cheaply and before I even started school I had access to those. Later there were frequent visits to Mtapa dumpsite- kuma Dee. There we would pick comics thrown away as trash from the white side of town. I use the term 'white side of town' to capture the racism that prevailed then. The comics were a treasure. These were comics on Chunky Charlie, She, Kid Colt, Captain Devil and many more.

Later in life I was to attend Muwunga Primary School. My mum dissatisfied with the standards there moved me and my young sisters to St Michaels Catholic Primary School. The formal education road then took me to the then prestigious Ascot School, Gweru 1979-82. I completed O level then. I then trained as a teacher at Andrew Louw Zintec College. Not satisfied I picked up books and went to ZDECO to do A Levels. I dropped out because I was not happy with the way I was being taught so I then studied on my own. I studied History, Literature in English and History. Having passed I looked elsewhere. I resigned as a teacher and became a trainee magistrate at the Judicial College of Zimbabwe. I was greatly incensed by the tag 'non degreed' magistrate. We had been recruited to fill the skills gap. There was an exodus of lawyers then. I then studied for a law degree with UNISA. During the same period I did a diploma in human resources management IPMZ. At fifty two I am not done yet. Watch the space!

What is poetry to you?

Poetry to me is painting pictures in words. It is organic in the sense that I draw from the socio-economic-political milieu I find myself in. The world in general provides the raw materials and I dig deep to find words that capture beauty, joys, sorrow and all human emotions, thoughts, dreams, etc. Like my late compatriot Dambudzo Marechera I have this firm conviction that 'Poetry is an attempt to put into words what is inside a person emotionally, intellectually, imaginatively. The poet's job is to find the equivalent, the verbal correlative of a particular feeling. This idea is from T S Eliot. The only difficulty is that there are no words for what you are feeling.' [Cemetery of Mind 1992:209].

Further poetry to me is prophecy, philosophy and a dive into the metaphysical realm too. It at times is therapeutic. After I have written a poem especially when the world seems to be collapsing around me I come away with renewed hope. That's magic drug.

What are the writers and artists that inspires you a lot, and why

There are many writers and artists that have greatly inspired me. These are too numerous to mention. Let me make mention of a few. Dambudzo Marechera- the great imagery and the lived experiences. David Mungoshi-the simple yet incisive works. Ummmmmm the recent work *Live Like An Artist* epitomises what I refer to. Nikolai Gogol, Dostoyesky, the Russians and great story telling. I recall the Great Coat by Nikolai Gogol. Harper Lee and how he tackles racism in *To Kill A Mocking Bird.* Of course I relate with the court scenes given my legal background. Charles Mungoshi is another writer whose works inspire me for the same reasons that David Mungoshi's works inspire me. My two Malawian brothers Jack Mapanje and Frank Chipasula are also grand masters of imagery. Further they also took the bull by the horns when Hastings Kamuzu Banda was at the helm for a long time in Malawi. Of course I protested artistically at what I saw as misrule in Zimbabwe when Robert Mugabe was at the helm for thirty-seven years! Reggae artists and dub poets inspire me greatly. I refer here to the voices of liberation of Mutabaruka, Benjamin Zephania, LKJ-Linton Kwesi Johnson. The redemption songs of Peter Tosh, Bob Marley, Bunny Wailer, Joseph Hill usually are background music as I write. I love the socio-economic-political commentary as I consider myself a revolutionary in the same mould as the reggae artists stated above and many more that sing of liberation from evil systems [shitstems] called Babylon.

You have written in both English and Shona, are they any other languages you write in. what do you find interesting in expressing yourself in many languages.

Predominantly I write in English and chiShona. English was the medium of instruction at school. ChiShona is my mother tongue. isiNdebele is what my late dad spoke. I am not very proficient in the language but I have a working knowledge. I have written very little in IsiNdebele. Ngiyakhuluma [I speak the language IsiNdebele] though! What is interesting is that I reach out to a wider audience when I write in the languages I refer to above. Like I said I paint pictures in words so at times one picture is better painted in ChiShona than in English. It is like sculpture. One may use soapstone and another may use marble or even metal to convey a message!

Your two poems in Zimbolicious Poetry Anthology Vol 1, "Yakarira Hwamanda Yechimurenga", and "Zvokwedu", are all in Shona. Tell us what they are about, what were the challenges of writing in this language, what was your translation process

The two poems are linked thematically in that they are taking about pride in our indigenous languages. Honestly I had no challenges that are out of the ordinary. I am bilingual. I was brought up by a Chishona speaking mother. That language is my mother tongue. Indigenous languages are equally rich and should not be allowed to die. The two poems speak to a cultural revolution. I am not saying we should abandon writing in English. No! Indigenous languages should get to the same pedestal as English! A lofty ideal! The translation process was quite difficult. I tried to get Mbizo Chirasha to do the translations. He was submerged by several projects. I then did the translations since I am bilingual basically. It was a challenge. I just then tried to capture the essence of the ChiShona poems as I translated. I think I managed to do so. I almost protested that I was losing the essence of what I had set out to do when I composed the poems in ChiShona. I however thought the editors wanted to reach out to a wider audience. Yes, very noble indeed.

Your two poems in Zimbolicious Poetry Anthology, Volume 2, the 2017 edition, "The Setting Sun", and "Another day" are both in English, tell us what these are about."

The setting sun is a prophetic poem to some extent. It predicted that the era of Mugabe's rule was coming to the end. The repression then made me resort to such imagery. The poem is therefore sort of multi-layered. Another day is a story of abject poverty where a girl goes begging to fend for her grandmother. There are the ever present dangers of sexual abuse. The child endures the vagaries of the weather as she goes about begging for the elusive United States Dollar. Oh I have another poem in that collection. It is entitled Murder Most Foul. It explores the issue of xenophobic attacks on Zimbabwean economic refugees in South Africa. That poem states that black South Africans are victims of thriving Apartheid pouncing on victims of misrule and so should see where the real enemy is.

Tell us about your forthcoming poetry book, "Under The Steel Yoke"

I am really excited that the collection may soon be published. There is not much that I wish to say about the yet to be published work. To whet prospective readers' appetites may I say the work comprises of poems composed when the poet felt that the revolution he supported and still supports was coming off the rails. The freedom train was becoming a gravy train. The majority wallowed in poverty and still do while a few politically connected went abroad to schools and flew to hospitals oversees and went to fashion capitals of the world for clothes. Cattle yokes are made of wood but the yoke we found ourselves under was made of steel. The rulers were driven by lack of altruism that had informed the liberation struggle. So the poems were composed during that dark, dank period. No publisher would touch the works. I was deemed anti-establishment but I refused to be labelled thus for I was conversely pro-establishment in the sense that I pointed out the derailment like Gogol and Dostoyevsky did in the Russia of old. So yes, the poems are protest poems like those of Mapanje and Chipasula during the iron fist, brutal rule of Banda.

Tell us about the writing scene in your country from since you started writing upto today

There was a time when BWAZ and ZIWU were quite vibrant. I met the likes of Shimmer Chinodya, Musonza, David Mungoshi, Willie Chigidi, Wiseman Magwa and many others. These organisations were instrumental in that some of us met the gurus in the field and looked up to them and got invaluable advice. There was a low cost poetry–prose magazine called Tsotso. Budding writers had a practising ground. I cannot forget the joys of seeing my work in print then. Then there was Moto Magazine. Now it lies in the grave yard of the publishing world. Moto had space for poets and short story writers. My work was featured too by that magazine. During the same period Ngoma Yokwedu was published by BWAZ in association with The Literature Bureau. I did contribute some work. Then the literary scene basically nose-dived. My view is that there is a lot of material

131

unpublished out there but the economic morass took its toll. Poetry suffered the most. I see a ray of hope though. The collection by my brother David Mungoshi was published by BHABHU BOOKS. I hope they will do more. As writers too we should endeavour to produce great works that merit publishing. Self -publishing is another way to go. My sister Virginia Phiri has done well in that area. All of us must also play our part in fostering a reading culture even for E-books. Zimbolicious poetry has also given us a great platform. More needs to be done.

You are a great fan of Reggae music, tell us about the artists you like, and how this music has inspired your writing

Oh yes maan. Reggae music I love. I will never understand/overstand any oppressed and colonised people who lack an appreciation for this music that basically talks of liberation/ emancipation. It is not bubble gum music. The lyrics of Bob Marley and Peter Tosh who passed on in 1981 and 1987 respectively remain poignant to this day. Truth, justice and equal rights are issues that reggae lyrics deal with largely. Yes the Rastaman can also be a lover par excellence. Listen to Gregory Isaacs and you will realise what I mean, maan. My work is inspired by the great reggae lyrics. I protest against oppression in much the same way that reggae artists do. I speak about truth, justice and equality. I hate oppression with a passion. Some of my works are spiritual. These are informed by the teachings of Rastafari and not a warped kind of Christianity that treats black people as sin and as hewers of wood and drawers of water.

At the home front, what kind of a person you are in the eyes of your family members

I am known as a speaker of the truth. I make some people in the family uncomfortable. I shoot straight. I have no sacred cows. I cannot sing praises where dirges are due. I have no time for control freaks and I tell them so. If your face is askew do not blame the mirror –Russian Proverb. The truth is like the sun, no man can look directly at it. I am a rebel against strictures at home, play or at the workplace. I am seen as a crazy man who writes but gets no royalties. I always quip that life has become so materialistic and one dimensional and we have become worshippers of mammon. I have repeatedly stated that I have inner satisfaction when I speak to the present and future generations. Yes I must put bread on the table but man shall not live by bread alone!

What are the improvements you want to see in the Zimbolicious poetry series in the future?

Improvements? The poems that one finds in Zimbolicious are of an exceptional quality. What needs to be done is to have these works available locally but like I said the economic malaise is a debilitating factor. One hopes books will be available locally at not so prohibitive cost.

Printed in the United States
By Bookmasters